Edith Stein
Philosopher and Mystic

THE WAY OF THE CHRISTIAN MYSTICS

GENERAL EDITOR

Noel Dermot O'Donoghue

Volume 12

Edith Stein

Philosopher and Mystic

by

Josephine Koeppel, OCD

A Michael Glazier Book
THE LITURGICAL PRESS
Collegeville, Minnesota

About the Author

Sr. Josephine Koeppel is a Discalced Carmelite nun at the Monastery in Elysburg, Pennsylvania. A native of Switzerland, she has translated the writings of Edith Stein for ICS Publications in Washington, D.C., and is recognized as an expert internationally on the life and work of Edith Stein.

A Michael Glazier Book
published by
THE LITURGICAL PRESS

Cover design by Placid Stuckenschneider, O.S.B.
Typography by Brenda Belizzone and Phyllis Boyd LeVane.

1   2   3   4   5   6   7   8   9

Library of Congress Cataloging-in-Publication Data
Koeppel, Josephine.
    Edith Stein : philospher and mystic / by Josephine Koeppel.
        p.   cm. — (The Way of the Christian mystics ; v. 12)
    "A Michael Glazier book."
    Includes bibliographical references and index.
    ISBN 0-8146-5625-0
    1. Stein, Edith, 1891-1942. 2. Carmelite Nuns—Germany-
-Biography. 3. Philosophers—Germany—Biography. 4. Mysticism-
-Germany—History—20th century. 5. Mysticism—Catholic Church-
-History—20th century. 6. Catholic Church—Doctrines-
-History—20th century. 7. Philosophy, Modern—20th century.
I. Title II. Series.
BX4705.S814K64 1990
271'.97102—dc20
[B]   90-62037
                                        CIP

Contents

Editor's Preface

Up to quite recently mystics were either misunderstood or simply not understood. But now we are coming to see that, in T.S. Eliot's words, the way of the mystics is "our only hope, or else despair." As the darkness deepens, and the lights go out, those ancient lights begin to appear and to show us the way forward. They are not only lights to guide us, but are each a human countenance in which we can recognise something of ourselves—each is a portrait for self-recognition.

Unfortunately, the great Christian mystics have been generally presented as models of perfection or monuments of orthodoxy—sometimes, too, as inhumanly joyless and ascetical. Yet they were, above all else, men and women of feeling, always vulnerable, at times perhaps insecure and uncertain of the way ahead. For all that, they all shine with a special divine likeness and a special human radiance.

Each of the following portraits tries to present a true likeness of its subject, a likeness that comes alive especially in the ordinary and the everyday. In each case the author has been asked to enliven scholarship with personal warmth, and to temper enthusiasm with accurate scholarship. Each portrait hopes to be in its own way a work of art, something carefully and lovingly fashioned out of genuine material.

The main focus nevertheless is on the way in which each mystic mediates the Christian Gospel, and so gives us a deeper, richer, clearer vision of the Christian mystery. This kind of exposition demands the reader's full and prayerful attention. Each book is the story of a pilgrimage, for the mystic, the writer and the reader.

Noel O'Donoghue

1

First Delineations—Edith Stein

Biography which in the course of time turns into hagiography poses a specific challenge which was not understood in the past. Perhaps literary style was partly to blame. However that may be, human beings must be seen as having human characteristics; portraying anyone as unrelievedly perfect is to offer a caricature to the observer and a slight to the person portrayed.

The story of an unforgettable person is given significant importance by the setting in which it is told. When an initial encounter is accompanied by an intense experience of wonder, or conversely, of pain and indignation, it will leave an indelible impression in the mind. When the first impression is confirmed, expanded, and shared, the groundwork is laid for a memorial in the heart. Giving the reader the experience of "discovering" Edith Stein, gradually, as the Carmelites in America did in the late 1940s, will lay a sound foundation for such a memorial.

A brief summary of the expansion of St. Teresa's Carmel from Spain into northern Europe sets the stage. St. Teresa's immediate "daughters", Anne of Jesus and Anne of St. Bartholomew, brought Carmel to Belgium one year after Carlotta of Urquine, daughter of Mateo de Urquine, Grand Chancellor to Philip III of Spain, was born in Brussels in June, 1606. Carlotta was received at the Carmel of Antwerp and made her profession as Sister Isabella of the Holy Spirit in 1630. Seven years later this very talented woman joined Mother Teresa of the Carmel of Brussels to bring the Order to

Germany. Mother Isabella was responsible for building the church in Cologne where the nuns live, again, today. Its Spanish architecture is a signature of this remarkable foundress' lineage.

The American Discalced Carmelite nuns first heard the story of Edith Stein, Sister Teresa Benedicta of the Cross, through correspondence with the Cologne nuns when a network of assistance was established between the American and European monasteries after World War II.

A letter written by Sr. Mechtildis in spring of 1946 was published by the Discalced Fathers of the Washington Province in their September/October issue of *Mount Carmel* magazine that year.

J.M. + J.T.

Cologne, Germany
May 14, 1946

Pax Christi!

Reverend and dear Fathers,

Whether this letter will arrive safely I do not know; however, I would like to attempt to give you some information regarding our city and our situation. A great sorrow has come upon us and God has afflicted our Fatherland severely. Never have Jeremiah's Lamentations been more suitable than today for our poor Cologne.

Since Pentecost 1940, enemy planes bombarded us day and night. The nights we spent mostly in the cellar. Many times our convent was hit by bombs and only with difficulty was the damage again scantily repaired, and the fire again extinguished. But during the attack of October 30, 1944, in which Lindenthal was hit the heaviest, enemy planes covered our Carmel with innumerable explosive and incendiary bombs.

Soon everything was in flames and we were able to leave the cellar only after the bombardment stopped. We went through the already burning cellar to the outdoors and a few minutes later the convent collapsed.

Unfortunately, our poor Sister Johanna of the Cross found her death in the flames. Even to this day, it has not been possible for us to find her remains. She is still buried under the wreckage as, indeed, are thousands in the devastated city. The entire Dürener Strasse, in which our Carmel lies, was a sea of flames and is today a place of debris and horror. Our entire furnishings of church and convent were burned, even into our cellars.

On November 5th, after a laborious and very dangerous journey, we came to Bavaria, where most of us found refuge in the Carmel at Theklaberg (Welden) into which we were lovingly received. Here we lived through the final horrors of the war. God miraculously saved and protected this convent. However, after the suspension of hostilities came the homesickness for the Rhine and for Cologne. By and by, the scattered nuns returned. There was no place to be found in this city of ruins; however, our Reverend Mother was able to rent a part of a damaged house (which is still being repaired) on the edge of the large city, in Cologne-Junkersdorf. Slowly we are all arriving here. We are housed very poorly and in close quarters and are unable to have either seclusion or a chapel. Three groups live in this house.

Our beloved Carmel is, like the entire street, totally and entirely destroyed. Reconstruction is out of the question. We are all destitute. Our sister-colleagues from Aachen, Düren, Echt, Luxembourg and Pützchen, who also were driven out of their convents, were able to return to their Carmel. Even if a few of their convents were damaged, they could, however, still live in them and rebuild everything. Only we poor Cologners are homeless.

To this is added the great need for food. Hunger reigns here and one is unable to get help.

Unspeakable misery lies behind us, and indeed, before us also. Therefore we need prayers and recommend ourselves to you at the Holy Sacrifice of the Mass and to your prayers.

Our Sister Teresia Benedicta a Cruce (Dr. Edith Stein), a Jewish convert, lost her life in a concentration camp. We have not heard any further details.

In the love of the Holy Hearts of Jesus and Mary, the
poor Carmelites of Cologne send greetings,

Sister Mechtildis
Cologne-Junkersdorf
Vogelsangerweg 43.

In subsequent correspondence, the nuns related how Sister
Teresa Benedicta of the Cross, for whom they continued to
grieve, had fled to Holland; how the Nazis had arrested her
there and sent her, with her sister Rosa, "to the east", presumably to their death. Her story was shared in the same spirit
in which an account of the long, hard struggle to rebuild a
monastery was being shared. Their ordeal inspired the American nuns to express both concern and interest. Continual
efforts were made to alleviate some of the Sisters' needs
through frequent shipments of the Care packages which are
part of World War II history.

Once the nuns were able to establish some regularity in their
life in Cologne, they set about, themselves, repairing the church
which had been built by Mother Isabella in the Schnurgasse in
1637. To this church, the Sisters were intent on attaching a
monastery to replace the ruins which had been the cradle of
Carmel for all of Germany.

Working as carpenters and masons, themselves, as there
were no laborers to be hired, the nuns appreciated all the more
the food packages which enabled them to keep on with the
strenuous work. In grateful and humorously labored English,
the sisters recounted their adventures in construction, and each
letter made an attempt to supply more personal information
about themselves and their Sister Teresa Benedicta.

In early autumn 1950, they sent a small tan booklet with but
twenty-four pages of German text. Its title, in red ink, identified
the essay as *Das Weinachtsgeheimnis* (The Mystery of
Christmas). In small print the author's name was given: Sr.
Teresia Benedicta a Cruce, then, the further identification:
Edith Stein. The prioress' request for its translation was the
beginning of years of work giving others access to Sr.
Benedicta's thoughts.

Two years elapsed before another text was received from

Cologne. This time it was *Lebensbild einer Philosophin und Karmelitin* (A Biography of a Philosopher and Carmelite Nun), written by Mother Renata de Spiritu Sancto (Posselt). Instructions were given to translate sections of the book and share them, in brief portions, with the community at the winter evening recreations. Since the autumn months of 1952, then, Edith's writings have been both occupation and inspiration.

When the American Carmelites received the first copies of "The Mystery of Christmas" in 1950, the nuns in Cologne were still without official word as to Edith's fate. Rumors and reports of sightings reached them but without substantive proof. They patiently followed up every clue, and inquired wherever there was the slightest chance of a trace or a connection to Edith or to her sister, Rosa Stein. Only in 1958, through the International Red Cross in Holland, was final certification of their death received.

By their correspondence with their sisters and brothers in the Order, the Cologne nuns made certain that Edith Stein's memory remained alive and that word about her spread wherever daughters of Teresa of Jesus can be found.

2

A Taste of the Spirit

When requests for information about her and, frequently, for some memento of Sister Benedicta continued to arrive at the Carmelite monastery after the war, the nuns realized how many persons remembered Edith Stein. Most of the Sisters' personal belongings, including articles Edith had worn or used, had either been blown up in earlier bombings, or were finally destroyed by the fire ignited by an incendiary bomb in October, 1944. Prompted by their own appreciation of Edith's spirituality, the nuns began to collect letters and memorabilia from her friends. Assured that these precious "things" would be preserved, those who had loved Fräulein Stein entrusted them to the community.

During her years in Cologne, Sister Benedicta had written a number of short essays on topics suggested to her for an upcoming feast or anniversary. "Mystery of Christmas" is among the best known. This meditation of Sister Teresa Benedicta's on the Incarnation was introduced to the readers of that 1950 issue by a foreword of Bishop Wilhelm Stockums of Cologne. On May 1, 1935, he had given the black veil of a finally professed nun to Sister Benedicta at Carmel, Cologne. Many of her faithful friends were present at that ceremony. On another memorable May 1, this time in 1987, Sister Benedicta was declared *Blessed* by Pope John Paul II in a ceremony attended by more than seventy thousand persons in Cologne's largest stadium.

Bishop Stockums commented in his opening words: "This booklet contains thoughts on the mystery of Christmas expressed in an exquisite manner by Dr. Edith Stein, who became the revered Carmelite, Sr. Teresa Benedicta of the Cross. It pleases me to introduce (this essay), first of all, because it is a truly deep and genuine religious exposition, and, also because I was personally acquainted with the author, having given her the veil on May 1, 1935, in the Carmel of Cologne-Lindenthal where, ten days earlier, she had made her perpetual profession.

"Dr. Edith Stein, Jewish by birth, was endowed with extraordinary gifts of spirit as well as of the heart; she was received into the Catholic Church on January 1, 1922, and on October 14, 1933, she entered the Carmelite Order in Cologne-Lindenthal. Her life and work held the highest promise but they were brought to a sudden, violent end in the Jewish persecution. Details of her life story are not all known at this date."

Bishop Stockum's tribute was written in Cologne, on June 19, 1948. After nearly forty years, the translation made from that first edition of the booklet remains one of the most poignant ways to become acquainted with the deep spirituality of Blessed Edith Stein. This series on the *Way of the Mystics* calls for references rather than for full translations of texts and so a few excerpts from "Mystery of Christmas" will suffice to show the beauty and depth of her thought.

Advent and Christmas

When the days grow progressively shorter, when (in a normal winter) the first snowflakes fall, then, timidly and softly, the first thoughts of Christmas steal into our hearts. The very word itself exerts a kind of magic and scarcely a heart escapes its charm. Even those of other creeds, even unbelievers for whom the age-old story of the Child of Bethlehem has no meaning, even these prepare for the feast and consider how, here and there, they can enkindle a warm ray of joy. It is as though a warm current of love inundates the world, weeks and even months before the time. A feast of love and happiness: this is the Star which attracts all humanity from winter's very first months on.

... In the ears of the one who holds the key to the inexhaustible treasure of Sacred Liturgy, the great Prophet of the Incarnation sounds his mighty exhortations and aspirations daily: "Drop down dew, ye heavens, and let the clouds rain the Just One." "The Lord is near! Let us adore Him!" "Come, Lord, and do not tarry." "Jerusalem, rejoice with great joy for your Savior is coming to you."

. . . Yes, when trees are candle-lit and gifts are exchanged on Christmas Eve, even then there is a yearning for another, a better Light, until the bells peal for Midnight Mass when, on the altar, decked with lights and flowers, the miracle of the Holy Night is renewed: "and the Word was made Flesh." This is the moment of sacred fulfillment.

The meditation then pictures the liturgical rather than the historical Court of the Infant King. Not only does Sister Benedicta reflect that although we have all had a taste of true Christmas joy, "still heaven and earth have not yet become one." She is aware that on the very day after Christmas, the Church commemorates Saint Stephen who was the first to follow the Lord in death. She sees the faithful Stephen in the company of the Holy Innocents standing near the Crib. She sees them forming the Child-King's royal entourage.

What does this tell us? Where now is the quiet jubilation of the heavenly angel hosts? Where is the quiet happiness of the Holy Night? Where is the peace on earth?

"Peace on earth to men of good will." But all are not of good will. That is why the Son of the Father had to descend out of the glorious Heaven, because the mystery of evil had shrouded the earth in night. Darkness covered the earth, and he came as the Light that shone in the darkness, but the dark did not comprehend him. He brought light and peace to those who received him: peace with the Father in heaven; peace with all others like them, children of light and children of the Father in heaven; and peace, the deep, interior peace of the heart; but not peace with the children of darkness. The Prince of Peace brought to these last not peace but the sword. To them he is a stumbling block, the rock against which they dash themselves to pieces. This is the hard and sober truth which may not be obscured by the poetic magic of the Child in the crib.

There is an association between the mystery of the In-carnation and the mystery of evil. Against the light which came down from heaven the night of sin stands out, all the more sinister and repulsive.

The Babe in the Crib stretches out his tiny hands and his smile seems already to say what the lips of the Man will later speak: "Come to me all you who labor and are heavily burdened."

These hands give and demand at one and the same time: "You, wise men, lay down your wisdom and become simple as children; you Kings, give up your crowns and bow down, humbly, before the King of Kings. Take upon you without a moment's hesitation the cares and pain and trials that his service provides! You children who are not yet able to give anything of your own free will, from you the infant hands accept your fragile lives even before they can rightly be said to have begun. Your life can be put to no greater use than this: to be offered up for the Lord of Life!"

"Follow me!" This is what the Infant's hands express just as later the lips of the Man would speak. Thus did the Lord address the disciple whom he loved and who now also belongs to the retinue at the crib. The young man with the pure heart of a child, St. John the Evangelist, did indeed follow without asking where or why. He left his father's boat and followed the Lord on all his journeyings until they reached Golgotha.

Sister Benedicta shows the differing ways in which each one found round the Crib followed the call. Then she reflects on the many others who should be there but who prefer the night of hardness and blindness of heart. But all this is not just applicable to Christ's contemporaries, for, as Edith tells us:

He is the King of Kings and the Lord of life and death. He speaks his "Follow me!" and whosoever is not for Him is against Him. He says it to us also and bids us choose between light and darkness.

Sister Benedicta next examines our relationship with one another in a section she entitles "The Mystical Body of Christ". She speaks of the universal call to union with God, and points out that those united to God in love, then, simultaneously, are joined in a common bond to all other human beings who have given their "yes" to God. This is not a sentimental bonding; it is in a sense a beginning on earth of the life of heaven where all are one in God.

> ... Our love for our fellow humans is the measure of our love for God. But it is different from a natural love of our neighbor. Natural love goes out to this one or that one, who may be close to us through the bond of blood or through a kinship of character or common interests. The rest then are "strangers" who "do not concern" us, who, it may be, eventually come to be repulsive, so that one keeps them as far away as possible from contact with us. For the Christian, there are no such "strangers". Rather, he is the "neighbor", this one who stands before us and who is in greatest need of our help; it matters not whether he is related to us or not; whether we "like" him or not; whether he is "morally worthy" of help or not. The love of Christ knows no bounds, it never stops, it does not shrink back from ugliness and dirt. He came for the sake of sinners and not for the sake of the just. If the love of Christ lives in us then we will, like Him, go out after the lost sheep.
>
> Natural love aims at completely possessing the beloved and if possible sharing him with no one else. Christ came to win back to His Father the lost humanity; and whosoever loves with His love wants to have persons for God and not for himself. In fact this is the safest way to keep them forever, for if we love a person in God and have entrusted him to God then we are one with him in God, whereas the desire to supersede all others often, indeed sooner or later always, leads to loss. What is thus applied to one's own soul applies also to the soul of the neighbor, even if he be a stranger to us. It applies to any outward good—whoever

outwardly seeks to win and to keep in possession, loses.
Whoever gives over to God, wins.

The third sign which identifies a child of God follows almost
naturally upon the other two. Union with God was the first;
that we are all one in God, the second. When Sister Benedicta
begins to speak of the third characteristic, she uses the language
in which she explains her own life with God. Anyone being
introduced to her spirituality will find in these concluding
reflections from her "Mystery of Christmas" the core, the heart
of the way of Edith Stein. The italicized sentences in what
follows are the "spiritual signature" of her message.

> ... *Being a child of God means to be led by the hand of
> God,* to do the will of God, not one's own, *to lay all care
> and all hope in God's hands,* to have no further care about
> oneself or one's future. Herein consists the freedom and
> happiness of the child of God. Yet how few, even of the
> most devout, even of those prepared to make heroic sacri-
> fices, possess it! They go on as it were bent down beneath
> the burden of their cares and duties. Everyone knows the
> parable of the birds of the sky and the lilies of the field. And
> yet, if they meet someone who, though without means,
> without a pension, without insurance, lives without a care
> for the future, they shake their heads as at an oddity. Of
> course, one who would look to God to supply a regular
> income and comfortable living conditions according to his
> individual taste would be sadly mistaken. Only then will
> trust in God stand firm when it includes a willing acceptance
> of all and anything from the hand of God. After all, He
> alone knows what is good for us. And if He deems need
> and privation more expedient at times than comfortable
> security, or when failure and humiliation come to us instead
> of honor and esteem—then we must be prepared to accept
> them. If one does so, then one can live without a care for
> the future.

This "Thy will be done!" in its fullest meaning must be the guiding line of the Christian life. It must rule the schedule of the day from morning until evening, the whole of the year, the whole of a lifetime. *In this case it becomes the one and only care of a Christian. All the other cares the Lord will take upon Himself. This one remains ours as long as we live.* Objectively, we cannot always be positively certain to remain constantly in God's ways. Just as the first humans could fall from sonship of God into estrangement from Him so do we all stand on the edge of the blade between night and the fullness of divine life. Sooner or later we are made to actually feel that this is the case. Whoever belongs to Christ must live the entire life of Christ. He must attain to the fullness of the age of Christ, yes, one day he must tread the way of the cross to Gethsemane and Golgotha. And all the suffering that comes from without is as nothing compared to the dark night of the soul, when the divine light no longer shines and the voice of the Lord no longer speaks. God is indeed here, but he is hidden and silent. Why must this be so? These are God's secrets of which we speak and we cannot completely understand them. But we do have a little insight into them. God became man that we might once more partake of His Life. That is the beginning and also the last goal.

But in between lies something else. Christ is both God and man, and whosoever would share His life must share both the Divine and the human life of Christ. The human nature that He took gave Him the ability to suffer and to die. The Divine Nature that He had possessed from all eternity gave to this suffering and death infinite value and redeeming power. The suffering and death of Christ continue in His mystical body and in each of His members. Every man must suffer and die. But if he is a living member of Christ's body, then his suffering and death, through the divinity of the head, receive redemptive power. This is precisely the reason why all the saints longed for suffering. This is not a morbid desire for pain. It may appear to the natural understanding as perversion. But in the light of the mystery of the redemption it is proved to be most highly sensible. That is why the soul that is united to Christ will endure even the darkest night of the passive estrangement from God and abandonment by Him without becoming disturbed. Perhaps the Providence of God has arranged this painful trial to set free a soul held captive. Therefore, "Thy Will be done"; and precisely therefore, in darkest night.

By this time in her life, Edith had not only lived her faith in Christ for more than a decade, she had led and directed many others to live according to her pattern. She calls her suggestions "remedies" for a number of spiritual ills. Again, it is clear that for her only one thing is necessary:

> But can we say "Thy will be done" even though we have no certainty of what God wants of us? Are there then means by which we may keep to His paths even when this interior light is extinguished? There are such means and such strong means that error on our part is by all principles improbable and forever impossible. For God came down to redeem us, to unite Himself with us, to unite us to one another, to conform our wills to His own. He knows our nature. He has reckoned on it and therefore He has given us all that can help us reach our goal.
>
> The Divine Child has become a teacher and has told us what we must do. Now to imbue an entire human life with the divine life, it is not enough, once a year, to kneel at the crib and allow oneself to be taken captive by the charm of the Holy Night. To do it, one must be in daily contact with God for the whole of one's life, hear the words which He has spoken, and which have been handed down to us, and obey them. Before all else, we must pray, even as our Lord Himself taught us, and as He impressed repeatedly, "Ask and you shall receive." This is positive assurance that we will be heard. So, whoever daily says, from his heart: "Thy will be done," can confidently trust that he will not fail to do God's will even when he lacks actual certainty of it.
>
> Furthermore, Jesus has not left us orphans. He has sent His Spirit who teaches us all truth: He has founded His church, led by His Spirit, and He has established in her His Vicar, by whose mouth the Spirit speaks to us in human

words. By means of the Church He has united all the faithful into one community and He wills that one should substitute for another. So we are not alone, and when confidence in our own judgement or even in our prayers is weak, then we are aided greatly by the strength of obedience and by the power of intercession.

"And the Word was made Flesh." This came true in Bethlehem's stable. But it has been fulfilled in another form. "Whosoever eats my Flesh and drinks my Blood, shall have everlasting life." The Savior who knows that we are human, and that we will always be human, that we must do battle daily with our human weaknesses, comes to our aid in a truly divine way. Just as our earthly body needs daily bread, so the divine life in us demands constant nourishment. "This is the living Bread which came down from Heaven." In the one who truly makes this his daily Bread, the mystery of Christmas, the Incarnation of the Word, is fulfilled daily. This then is the surest way in which union with God will become lasting, in which we grow daily deeper and more firmly into the mystical body of Christ. I know quite well that this desire will seem to many people to be quite radical. Practically speaking it means, for many who are only beginning, a complete change in their interior and exterior life. But that is just exactly what it should be! To make room in our life for the Eucharistic Savior so that He may transform our lives into His life: is that asking too much? There is time in our life for so many useless things: reading together all kinds of unnecessary matter out of books, magazines, and newspapers; sitting in cafés; wasting fifteen or thirty minutes gossiping on the street: all "distractions" in which time and energy are splintered. Is it really impossible to spare one hour in the morning in which one does not distract but rather recollects oneself, in which one is not exhausted but rather gains strength with which to do battle the whole day?

But of course, there is more to it than just the one hour. One has to live from one such hour to the next in a manner that will permit one to come again! One may no longer "let yourself go" even for a time. We cannot escape the criticism of those with whom we associate daily. Even though no single word is spoken, we sense how they feel about us. We try to adapt ourselves to our surroundings and should this become impossible then living together becomes intolerable. Something similar happens when we are in daily contact with our Savior. We become ever more sensitive to what pleases or displeases him. If, before, we were, on the whole, well satisfied with ourselves, now all is different. We find so much that is flawed, and to the extent of our capability, we will amend. Then we see other things about ourselves that we cannot call nice or good, yet they are difficult to change. This gradually makes one become little, and humble; one becomes patient and overlooks the mote in others' eyes because the beam in one's own eye gives us plenty of work. Then, finally one learns to endure the sight of oneself in the inescapable light of the Divine Presence, and to abandon oneself to the Divine Mercy which is able to accomplish all that defies our strength. It is a long, long way from the self-complacency of the "good Catholic" (who fulfills his duties, who reads a good newspaper, who votes right, etc., etc., but otherwise does much as he pleases) to the *living at God's hand, receiving all from him in the simplicity of a child and the humility of the publican.* But *whoever has once taken this way will never turn back on it again.*

This is translating the Gospel message of Christ, practically, into the every day life of a Christian. Whoever fosters a daily Eucharistic contact with the Lord will stop being centered on self, and be concerned with the Lord's interests. The concluding reflections which Sister Benedicta gave in her "Mystery of Christmas" apply the lessons she learned from the liturgical year of the Church to our own situation, today. We are now ready to meet in person this Carmelite nun whose life has been an inspiration to cradle Christians and even more to those who find their way into the Church in adult life. Did Edith Stein's private life in childhood and early youth lead one to expect her future role among Christians? Only when one remembers that God's ways are often inscrutable and that his plans for us bear the full imprint of his love for us.

3

Begin As You Mean To Go On

In our sophistication, we seldom fall back on proverbial statements to understand what is happening in our lives. However, anyone intimately familiar with maxims handed down through centuries in more than one culture knows how uncannily folk wisdom can crystallize a thought. In studying God's ways with his friends, it also pays to keep the advice of the biblical writers in mind, for they are right on target in most cases. Following the "way" of our lives as indicated by such repeatedly used signposts erected on our path by God enables us to "see" His role in the lives of his friends. In Edith Stein's life, God himself "began as he intended to go on"—eventually, she arrived at an active acceptance of all from his hand, but from the very beginning, he provided all she needed in the face of every event of her life.

The story of Edith Stein's life is best read in her own account. When Erich Przywara, the Jesuit theologian, urged her, at the time when Hitler was beginning to show the perverted plan he meant to pursue, to write about life in a Jewish family, it was not Edith's intention to produce an autobiography. But God was merely continuing to direct her way just as had done all her life. Before she could herself be aware of it God had given Edith a hunger and thirst for truth. He left to her own initiative and insatiable energy the efforts she would make to discover that truth, to search out its meaning, and then to live it out at every phase of her life.

Edith Stein was beautifully human with a remarkable balance of traits which people alternately admired or found irritating! Her relatives and friends knew how deeply she was committed to the truth as she sought it both in them and in herself. They considered some of her actions or decisions far from perfect, even wrong. She often needed time to ponder a matter before she was certain of her course; that her ultimate resolution met with misunderstanding or opposition from colleagues or friends and relatives is ample proof of her being normal.

Normal too was God's relationship with Edith Stein. He did not wait until her mature years to appeal to her love. Still a child, she responded without being aware that the truth toward which she was so attracted was leading her toward Divine Truth. Only many years later did she realize that her whole life had been an "unrelenting search for truth". This search led her to three plateaus along her way: first, truth was found in facts; then in persons, and, finally, in God.

Edith Stein's gifted intelligence was awakened at an early age under the stimulus of her siblings' tuition. Religious instruction alone fell short of the excellence available to her in secular educational subjects. Outside the family there was no systematic initiation into the "faith of her Fathers." This circumstance must be kept in mind and weighed against Edith's statement that at the age of fifteen she "lost the faith she had as a child". What she did lose was in large part an uninstructed faith which prevented her from discovering the depth and riches of Jewish beliefs during her childhood and adolescence.

So, with little spiritual food to satisfy her hunger for truth, it is not surprising that Edith put her confidence into "facts" such as her brother Paul eagerly taught her. Several years and much inner pain and puzzlement brought her to realize that life offered more than dry information. Gradually, she began to withdraw her attention from the merely factual to concentrate on finding a meaning to life.

Young as Edith was, she assumed responsibility for her own development. This, naturally, proved to be a disadvantage. Her experience armed her with little by way of alternatives, so she made the best of a difficult situation.

When she recounted the events of her childhood in her *Life in a Jewish Family*, Edith's principal concern was to portray day to day events in her mother's home. But her faithful account also discloses that in those early years she learned to bear a great deal of hidden pain. The protracted absence at work of her mother, in whom Edith would naturally have confided, led her to be silent about many troubling matters. Indeed, she says she came to assume one did not talk about them. But normal child that she was, the little "Jitschl," as she called herself, exhibited the natural result of such constraint. From her unexplained fevers, severe enough to cause her to be confined to bed where in a kind of delirium she spoke of her deep concerns, her relatives perceived that life for this sensitive little girl was not always easy.

By pre-adolescence, Edith learned that meaning had to be taken into consideration as well as straightforward facts. Gradually, meaning was to expand; still, only during her university years would she admit to a call for a commitment to the truth of life's spiritual component.

The denial of the spiritual when she was fifteen years old, the conscious choice not to believe in a God, had been deliberate. So was her conclusion not to pray any longer: if there is no God, there can be no prayer. Yet, God used no extraordinary means to jolt her out of her tremulous independence. He merely let her see what faith in action represented.

In 1917, her dear friend and mentor, Adolf Reinach, was killed in World War I; his widow called upon Edith to help with putting his scholarly writings in order. On that visit to Frau Reinach, Edith experienced for the first time the power of the Cross and the role of faith: together, they enabled the widow to accept her shattering loss and to share her own hope and peace with Edith. For the young philosopher, a door opened which she was never again to close.

After a quarter of a century of searching for truth, Edith was ushered into the phase of *living* it. Her search ended with the reception of the Sacrament of Baptism which she received on New Year's Day, 1922. That day the liturgical calendar of the Church commemorated the Circumcision of the Infant Jesus.

Confirmation was administered to her on February 2nd, when the Church annually keeps the remembrance of another Jewish ritual celebration in the life of Jesus, his presentation in the temple forty days after his birth. Edith herself may have chosen the dates for the reception of the initial sacraments particularly because of their scriptural ties to Jewish customs. At the time of her Baptism, Edith was convinced that her way led into a Carmelite monastery where the life of contemplative prayer would be the fulfillment of her baptismal commitment. As she conformed to the wishes of her spiritual guides and postponed thoughts of Carmel, she nevertheless discovered her own formula for living the vocation, in anticipation, as it were. This can only be recognized when one looks back over her lifestyle in those years, 1922 to 1933, and listens to her recipe for daily living, as we have found it in her essay on Christmas.

This was that third phase of her relationship with truth. Edith placed her life and all its circumstances, without reservation, at God's disposal. This was her particular grace: to recognize that all that was required of one was to accept all from God's hand. True acceptance, of course, meant including, without demurring, the *consequences* of this receptive attitude. When friends and well-meaning advisors suggested more learned topics for her lectures, and intimated that her favorite might be ignored once in a while, she made it clear that whatever might be expected of her, she *had* to include the one truth by which she was now living: all comes to us from God and we are asked to accept it from Him.

Eleven years of this kind of acceptance, especially of being kept from her dream of entering a Carmelite monastery, earned for Edith a harvest of blessings for her students and her listeners. Even as a teacher and lecturer, she could practice the single-heartedness which would characterize her life as a religious.

God's providence did send some consolations during that long period of waiting. Both in Speyer and Münster, she was able to find lodging in convents so that her surroundings and her daily schedule were nearly those of a Carmelite.

Edith's gratitude was but a preface to the satisfaction she experienced upon entering the monastery of the Discalced Carmelite Nuns in Cologne in October, 1933. She said:

> God kept something for me in Carmel which I had not found anywhere else.

Precisely what was meant by this "something" was never fully disclosed since Edith felt it was a secret between God and herself. We know, in part, it meant she was completely accepting of all from God's hand in the final years of her life despite their increasingly painful developments, but that had already been her practice. In Carmel, however, even her lifestyle expressed this total gift of self, keeping nothing back for her own disposition. So radical an emptying of herself she had found nowhere else.

Carmel, the brief form of the name of the Order of Our Lady of Mount Carmel, was ideal for Edith. Like that of her forebears, the history of the Order is bound up with the history of Israel, of the patriarchs and prophets, especially Elijah, and so also with Abraham, the father of faith. Belief in Jesus, the son of David and the son of God, recapitulated all the rest. As we learn from her own writings, Edith Stein's Jewish heritage meant as much to her as her German citizenship.

During her years of studying, caring for wounded soldiers, and lecturing, it was Edith's common practice to tell persons who were unaware of it that she was Jewish, should the topic come up in their conversation. She found it interesting and, at times, even amusing, to note how frequently people were surprised by her statement. With classmates or friends who shared that heritage, she felt a bond which meant much to her; mutually, they would be delighted when they found another whom they could count as "one of us". This loyalty remained with her until the very end, when the most comforting and strengthening phrase she could think of as Rosa and she were arrested, was: "Come, let us go for our people."

This Jewish identity was important to her; she was always comfortable in owning it. Any others who were apologetic or reluctant to say anything about their heritage knew that in her presence they should be open about it. One consequence of her quiet, unobtrusive presence was that she found wherever she went, persons attracted to her to whom everything about her was just as they would have wished. Today, although we search for her in round-about ways, we have the same experience. The response upon the discovery of her forthrightness, warmth, and understanding of human nature is one of real satisfaction. At the same time, her deeply spiritual characteristics are revealed.

How did she attain to all of this? Following her account of her life through each of the three phases in her search for truth will allow us to trace God's work and her cooperation, progressing from a strict adherence to truth through the ways of knowing herself and other persons, to her meeting with God, until we find her simply resting in Divine Truth which spells beatitude, true blessedness.

4

The First Gift:
Life in a Jewish Family

Edith was born in Breslau, then in Germany, now part of Poland, on October 12, 1891. That it happened to be the Day of Atonement seemed to her mother, Auguste Stein, a mark of God's special love for the child and for herself.

As the youngest of the Stein siblings, Edith was surrounded from the first by a family of devoted grown-ups. Four other Stein children had died in infancy. Only Erna, not quite two years Edith's senior, shared childhood with Edith. The rest of her sisters and brothers were no longer considered children, but had assumed the tasks and responsibilities of young adults.

As a child, Edith was naive in her conviction that she was both the star in the play of life and its director. From the beginning, however, it is clear that God patiently and skillfully added emphasis, introduced counterpoint, or ended a strong theme whenever this was required in the symphony of her life. The stage for the first dramatic intervention was set on a warm, sunny day in July, 1893.

Edith's father, Siegfried Stein, was to make one of his frequent buying trips to Upper Silesia. At fifty, he managed to handle the many aspects of his lumber business without any problems. At least, that seemed to be so. This day, he was to visit some property where a healthy stand of trees looked promising: perhaps the most arduous aspect of the trip was having to walk so many miles. This was for him the only mode of travel in the rural area where rail service was unavailable.

The Steins could not afford a team and wagon; their deliveries of wood to customers were made on a dog-drawn cart.

The sheer physical stress awaiting him may have caused him to be abrupt rather than buoyant as he set out that July morning. Whatever the circumstances of that leave-taking, there was an intervention by the two-year-old Edith which her mother gratefully mentioned whenever the family reminisced about Siegfried's departure on the trip from which he would not return.

When Siegfried set out for Frauenwaldau, Auguste took the tiny "Jitschl" on her arm as she accompanied her husband to the door. When he had gone but a few steps, the baby imperiously called him back for another farewell embrace. That was an unusual enough occurrence to etch the scene on Frau Stein's mind; she looked on Edith as a legacy received from Siegfried as he set out finally.

Hours later, his death, possibly from a heat-stroke, was discovered by a rural postal employee who had seen a man reclining under a tree in the morning and noticed upon his return down that country lane that the man had not changed position in any way.

Suddenly, life for the Stein family changed beyond expectation. When Frau Stein went to bring back the body to Breslau she closed a chapter in Edith's life though neither of them were aware of the significant step taken by them all in their life in God's hand.

Extensive changes in the household on Kohlenstrasse resulted. They were to affect the two youngest daughters most directly. They lost more than a devoted father and the influence he would have had on their education. Erna and Edith, from that time on, were deprived of their mother's constant presence and of her patient, irreplaceable instruction in housekeeping. Frau Stein set off for the lumberyard at first light and the little ones often did not see her until she returned home at the onset of dusk. Having put in such long hours of labor with her workers, Auguste was too weary to do more than take her youngest children along to bed. Pleasant as that was, it did not offer much opportunity to ask the endless questions that children puzzle over. Taking a cue from their older siblings, Erna and Edith learned to keep the evening hours as restful for their mother as they could.

As though to symbolize the many changes affecting the Steins, Auguste decided to move her brood to a larger apartment in a location more convenient for her daily trek to the lumberyard. Edith retained only one memory of her years in the house where she was born. It was of a white door, closed and impregnable, and of herself fiercely drumming on that door and screaming because her eldest sister Else was on the other side of it, and the tot wanted to be with her.

Superficially, the incident was dismissed as an ill-mannered tantrum of a spoiled two-year-old. From Edith's comment one can deduce that was the most natural interpretation of her behavior. However, an alternative explanation for the child's panic exists.

How capable is a two-year-old of realizing what death means in one's experience? If she recalled her father's final farewell, might the child Edith have continued to expect and await a father who failed to come? Did it occur to her that out-of-sight meant never-to-return-again sometime? It was a lesson to be learned, remembered, and immediately acted upon in need. A door that refused to open was such an emergency and called forth screams for her sister Else to come back.

Edith had a remarkable gift for recounting in great detail what lay behind many of her actions and decisions. She has established a fund of information on childhood and children hard to find in the writings of the other Carmelite authors.

Only years later did the full meaning of her stories occur to her. God had been the storyteller down through the years. That, Edith came to believe, is true for everyone's life. Her understanding of a person's individual history made her say, later, that one of the joys she looked forward to in heaven would be to get to know the full stories of individual lives. She took a vital interest in developments in the lives of those around her.

The mobility of Edith's family makes her story accessible to single parents, or to latch-key children whose experiences today are very similar to Erna's and Edith's. Three times in less than four years, for instance, the family moved into new living quarters. The changes were hardly made at whim; to move with children was a formidable enterprise taken only as a last resort.

Edith outlines her life in those early years: she and Erna spent a large part of their pre-school days alone in the apartment. They had stringent orders never to admit strangers. The little ones had a strong code of honesty; Edith assures us that if there was reason to be naughty or disobedient, they followed the urge only if their mother was present.

The home on Jägerstrasse was also the place where Edith's earliest and formative peer experiences are recorded. True, Erna was almost two years older, but the two had always been together and were much like twins. They needed other companionship against which to measure and develop skills in communicating, leadership, and compatibility. Numerous cousins and the children of other tenants in the apartment building all had access to Frau Stein's lumberyard as a playground.

It is evident from the enjoyment Edith found with so many companions in play that she was not egocentric; a spoiled child would have resented this intrusion on her personal playground. There were no attempts on the part of either of the Stein youngsters to establish a territory to which admission was granted to a favored few; instead, with their mother's help and supervision, they accepted and shared friendship and played with all who came, and kept a protecting eye on even younger children whose safety in the busy lumberyard required that they be watched.

At this early stage in Edith's life, she began to exhibit publicly the highest individual trait her family had noticed and remarked upon. The child was absolutely dedicated to truth: she was intent on finding it, learning all about it. When she was sure of something—when she knew it to be true—she could not be budged from it by any means.

Edith, a sturdy little girl, was determined to keep the record straight. Insisting that those around her conform to her standards, she did not hesitate to make it clear if any hapless person in her presence expressed an idea or a belief which diverged from some reality stored in her ever expanding fund of knowledge.

In the opinion of her proud and delighted relatives, because of her intelligence and tenacity, Jitschl was the perfect candidate for teasing. They persisted in efforts to confuse her about things she learned from her big brother Paul. Too small to realize that these misinformed claims of theirs were but stage settings arranged for her to display her talents, Edith lost patience with them. What was she to do with these aunts and uncles who could not identify a book's author correctly and, worse, who refused to take her word for the truth until she clarified their mistakes beyond doubt?

The child could not have expressed what was happening in her quest for knowledge. Her knowing far exceeded her understanding. Edith recognized truth but did not know why it was true. She was confident about her conclusion, her decisions. Her priority was truth in every instance. In some sense, a relationship, an exchange of goods, was taking place between her and the God who is truth. But he remained hidden, not in the learning she had imbibed, but in her love for what was true. Only later did she know how He had identified himself as truth. In her search for knowledge, she was on the way to God, and in her clinging to truth when and where she encountered it, she was relating to God.

In her own words, she recognized what had happened to her as a universal experience: "Whoever seeks truth is seeking God whether they are aware of it or not."

Truth for the child Edith was wrapped in words; they became all-important through her insatiable hunger for knowledge. By expressing the truth as she saw it, roundly, and if pressed, vociferously, she came to appreciate words as the ornament, the armor, and frequently the burden of an articulate soul. That mysterious aura to words which clothes the truth in them was something she was still too young to identify. She came close, however, to worshipping it; and no wonder this was so, for we read in Scriptures that from the very beginning of creation there was a Word, and the Word was God. Never an impatient God, he was content to allow her to find her way to the fulness of understanding. In the meantime, through the joy she experienced in her quest, he was allowing her a share in his own joy.

Edith's childhood, though full of opportunities for play and learning, had its abundant share of trials. Sometimes a description of violence, or a conversation in the family about an unpleasant situation, or, perhaps, caught at a window, a fleeting glimpse of a very inebriated passerby, would upset Edith, disturbing her sleep and her waking reflections for days on end. When she wrote about those years of her life, she recalled her feeling of helplessness, her lack of a confidante, her being at the mercy of endless, depressing thoughts.

Occasionally, even something which should have given her great joy developed instead into a painful experience. Mothers in Breslau took their youngsters for a stroll around the Ring, the center of all activity in the town. Because of Frau Stein's heavy work schedule, Erna and Edith seldom got to go on promenade and so they appreciated all the more an invitation to join a playmate and her mother, one lovely day.

The children made the arrangement themselves. The Stein sisters would go home to put on their best dresses, since a walk at the Ring meant being seen by lots of people. The little friend and her mother would meet them at the appointed time and the treat would be underway. However, in the excitement, the little girls failed to agree on the meeting place. Dressed and eager, Erna and Edith waited to be called for at home, while their youthful "hostess" was confident that they were to come to her house. The inevitable result of the confusion was that the only adult involved decided that if anyone at all were to have a walk, she and her little daughter better go alone as usual.

When Erna and Edith saw their friend the following day, it was Edith, the youngest of the trio, who made her feelings known beyond doubt. "Once a person is caught telling an untruth, they are never believed again!"

This kind of painful experience creates an attitude toward relationships with others which is extremely important. Since the details are usually embarrassing they do not become public knowledge and some catalytic event is needed for such a private feeling of betrayal to come out into the open. Edith Stein's gift for story-telling, her empathy, and her reliability enable the reader to take instruction from the anecdotes she recounts in order to understand, because of her openness, her growth through pain. Extraordinary happiness, joy and love are powerfully maturing; but pain widens the heart, provided it does not leave behind a bitterness bred from ignorance.

Perceptive enough to be aware of her mother's burdens,

Edith was determined not to add to them, just as she and Erna, aware that the family had to stretch every resource, hesitated to ask for anything that was an added expense. But suppressing all this turmoil with an imagination and temperament such as Edith had could only cause trouble. Edith's behavior became erratic.

The youngest member of the Stein family was subjected to close scrutiny by her relatives who compared observations whenever they discussed Auguste's brood. Jitschl was as restless as quicksilver, precocious and full of pranks, with a stubborn will and a temper which earned her a reputation in the extended family.

What was not observed, though, was the hidden world within the childish heart where all her experiences were mulled over. There the pleasant happenings were savored, but far more, the unpleasant ones were allowed to haunt and plague the little girl until inexplicable fevers and distressing nightmares drew attention to the overburdened but valiant little spirit.

Edith had only one pillar to lean on in her struggle to overcome fear. She placed her confidence in whatever she could call "true". Surprisingly, this effort to gain self-mastery seemed to succeed, and she came to depend solely on her own evaluation of everyday situations. One mistake undermined the effort; she was prone to believe that everyone else was guided by the same principle. This was evident when she accepted another's statement without skepticism or doubt.

Else, her eldest sister, returned to teachers college once Frieda took over the management of the house. When the time came for her examination, Else startled her youngest sisters by declaring a failure in the test would "drive her into the river."

On examination day, Else had not returned from the long day's ordeal by bedtime for the two children. Frau Stein tucked them in with a firm promise to wake them when Else came home. That young lady, in high spirits at putting the test successfully behind her, decided to deceive the little girls.

At her suggestion, Frau Stein bent over Edith who was fully alert at the first sound: "Just think, Jitschl, Else failed her test." In a moment, the child had leaped from bed, and with arms flung around Else's neck, begged in tears: "Oh, Else, promise you won't go in the river! Promise!"

When the same dire report was given, next, to Erna, who was sound asleep, she simply muttered, "Tell me another one." With that, she was back in dreamland.

Puzzled by such behavior and unable to discuss it, the child, Edith, stored away such experiences for pondering. The conviction grew in her that school had to be the answer to all her problems. School was a marvelous place: teachers spent whole days there for no other reason than to tell the students things they did not yet know!

The time came when Erna was admitted to this halcyon place. The protest came from Jitschl's heart. Why, why was she not allowed to go along with Erna? Were they not always together at home and was it not a sure thing that Edith knew everything Erna did? How was she ever to "learn" anything if they denied her the right to go to the *big* school?

Persistence was rewarded. Edith, on her sixth birthday, was received at mid-term at the Victoria School in Breslau. She embraced her new "state" confident that now she would be able to satisfy her every desire for truth; it was all there awaiting her. Edith's years at the Victoria School in Breslau were devoted to simply soaking up every bit of knowledge that came her way.

However, there was a milestone to mark this phase of Edith's journey toward truth. She described it herself as a "transformation" which took place when she was about seven years old. It was, she says, sudden and interior, and took the form of a conviction that her mother and her eldest sister had a better knowledge about what was good for Edith than she had herself.

That a youngster recalls so vividly an attitude that brought about a radical change in her behavior is not unusual, but that the thing be simply a conclusion drawn out of the subconscious is worthy of note. And the most important consequence is that it was a first, clear proof of Edith's fidelity to truth. Since she was convinced they knew best, she followed their wishes; actions were for her the necessary confirmation of her inner attitude.

A second seven years passed before there was another kind of transformation. Edith, always an energetic student, was suddenly convinced that she had had enough of school. Her decision took the family by surprise. Only a few years ago, Edith had begged with tears and with tantrums to go to school; now she calmly informed them she was taking off for Hamburg to spend some time with her eldest sister, Else. Her elder siblings felt obliged to talk her 'around,' but Edith found an ally in her mother. Even though she was the youngest, Frau Stein told her grown-up sons and daughters, Edith had the privilege of deciding for herself, just as all her seniors had done.

So she said good-bye to books, and set out for Hamburg and the home of the Gordons where she found a sincere welcome. Else was about to have her second child, and it was a delight to have her youngest sister come as "mother's help".

The move to Hamburg marks a turning point in Edith's life in more than one significant way. No longer would she be Jitschl, for in the city, no one would be so unkind as to address her by her childhood name. It almost seemed that a mantle of dignity fell on these young shoulders, and under it, during her stay in Hamburg a young lady came into existence.

An all-important interior change in Edith had taken place in the final months of her school years. It would have shocked Frau Stein, had she been aware of Edith's attitude. But since she had never been her youngest's confidant, she was unaware of Edith's cool, deliberate decision to give up prayer since she no longer believed in God. The change did not show in her comportment. It was a silent declaration of independence, when Edith seemed no longer to trust reason, or facts from books, nor, any longer, her elders.

It was almost as though Edith suspended her judgement and then acted accordingly. Having made a conscious choice of a position toward faith, there was no more hesitation on Edith's part. She was free of plans for a future, free of tasks in the present, once school at the Victoria had ended, and she shook herself free of any residue of a past that might make her feel either regret or responsibility. What was to be, would be. Edith, the fifteen year old sage, became more of a spectator to life than a participant.

5

Truth Wears Human Features

Leading a twin existence for siblings who are not twins may temporarily cause one of them to lose the healthy individual sense which has been subjugated to the value of alikeness that has such an appeal in childhood. The first break with "doing what Erna was doing" came when Edith decided to discontinue her schooling.

The decision interrupted more than Edith's studies. The social life in the Stein home was lively, most of its activity taking place in the family circle. So, when she decided to go to Else's, she was also choosing to exchange the pleasant existence she enjoyed in her mother's home for a lifestyle to which she was not accustomed. In Hamburg, where they had no other relatives, her contact with persons outside the Gordon home would be limited.

In Else's home, Edith had clear responsibilities. She is content to say that her brother-in-law, after an initial surprise that someone so young and inexperienced was expected to do so much, was well satisfied with her performance as housekeeper and nursemaid for her sister and for the two children.

Dr. Gordon expressed concern about Edith's welfare on several occasions; one cannot but be surprised, then, at his apparent obliviousness to Edith's recreation while she was in his house. She was reading the medical books and journals in his library. Edith contents herself thirty years later with the comment that, in Hamburg, she read many things not meant for a fifteen year old girl.

And from the unembroidered and frank account she gives of Else's conversations in those ten months in Hamburg, Edith had an intimate glimpse of her eldest sister's marital situation. At the same time, she was aware that Max and Else had a deep need and love for one another and in the opinion of the silent witness to their difficulties, their love only made their frustrations more painful.

Edith was not naive; all the painful misunderstandings she witnessed did not make her cynical or dissuade her from thinking of marriage herself. It did bring her to formulate her own ideals for a husband and wife relationship which she eventually equated with what she called the "Catholic ideal" for a happy marriage.

Her return to the maternal hearth was brought about by the critical illness of her baby nephew, Harald. He died within days of her return. Edith was more introspective than before her Hamburg sojourn. Coming into close contact with relationships which had been outside her experience during her first fifteen years gave her an object lesson on life's serious side. Soon, however, she resumed her customary place in the family as though she had never gone away. However, it did seem strange to be around the house all day. She, who had clamored so vociferously to be allowed to go to school a decade earlier, now watched Erna go off each morning to her pre-med classes.

Helping Erna, even at times accompanying her to a lecture, reawakened in Edith a taste for textbooks. Why only be of help to Erna? The thought kept cropping up that the time and effort should be invested in her own future. When she returned to classes in the Obersekunda in Breslau in 1908, she herself had changed remarkably. Only her determination to make the best of every single day had not altered. She easily made up the year she had missed. With excellent marks, she continued her studies as preparation for attending the University of Breslau. Leaving her teen years behind, Edith began attendance at the university when the summer semester of 1911 began on April 27.

This new chapter in her life signalled a deeper change in her personality. What she recorded of those years shows clearly that circumstances no longer held center stage. Edith's search for truth was continuing but it was now focusing on people. Education was no less important than before, but it was no longer a matter of accumulating factual knowledge. For Edith, courses in the years ahead were of interest because they taught her about life which fascinated her.

Her views on pedagogy, on the obligations and responsibilities of teachers show beyond doubt that she based her opinions on her experience, having tested the truth of her theories against her own success or difficulty in relationships with teachers and students.

We have repeated evidence that Edith learned from her own mistakes, and put the knowledge gained from experience at the service of others. Her Breslau school years were responsible for her later views on pedagogy, especially with regard to curricula in the girls' schools. She was convinced that it was vitally necessary to keep students' future duties and interests in view when planning their courses.

When in later years her position enabled her to influence educators at all levels, she presented her argument that only women could competently plan the education of girls. She had the best interests of the students at heart; it was not a matter of choosing a brilliant program of studies, but of providing what would be of the greatest assistance to each girl in her private preparation for adult life.

Two extraordinary events took place during her second year at the University of Breslau. They almost seem to be mysterious dress rehearsals of future events.

Until her sister Erna married, Edith shared a bedroom with her at home in Breslau. Tragedy brushed them very closely one night. They had turned low a gas lamp in their room; too low, for the flame died while they slept. But for their sister Frieda's timely and horrified intervention, the two girls would have been asphyxiated.

Edith never forgot her spontaneous, semi-conscious reaction when she was awakened. She knew a keen regret at not being allowed *to sleep on in such great peace!* Her surprise was sharp: "I did not know how little I clung to life!"

Years later, no one could intervene when the gas was turned on at Auschwitz. Nor was there an aura of peace surrounding that experience. Yet, for those who cherish Edith, the thought of these incidents when juxtaposed has a terrible sense of deja vu.

The second event reveals Edith's intense involvement in her environment. As a child, imaginary episodes could cause fevers and nightmares—now, eight years in advance of the most painful period in her private life, she was made ill by internalizing the feelings awakened by a novel which portrayed uncannily parallel circumstances of "university life". For us, in this case, hindsight can be prophetic. We can gauge the depth of the pain of the real-life experience when we read that she agonized over a fictional situation so intensely as to cause a physical illness.

Edith was twenty-one years old when she read the novel *Helmut Harringa*. That the mere reading of a book should cast Edith into a state of deep depression and illness against which she was completely helpless seems, at first, an incredible over-reaction to a piece of fiction. It does give a remarkable insight about her spiritual sensitivity. The literature of Germany and of Austria, at this time, was eminently suited to depress readers. Almost across the board, poets and novelists under the influence of naturalism, reinforced with touches of proud individualism and of character weakness that refused to face reality, produced works which inundated society with pessimistic gloom. The solutions they presented were destined to affect the lives of the young in all too often tragic ways.

In Germany, since Goethe's time, nearly a century and a half before Edith's experience, so many young people imitated his *Werther*'s cowardly decision to end his own life that the phenomenon of copycat suicides is today known as the Werther syndrome. The opening decade of the twentieth century was marred by another epidemic of suicides, first in literature, then, unfortunately, in real life.

Since society learned little from the former tragic cycles, history merely repeated itself in ever tighter circles. Today, one again reads of "clusters" of young suicides. Such incidents cause a great deal of suffering to young and old, to anyone who loses a relative or a friend so needlessly. The frank description of the intense pain which, as Edith Stein admits, eclipsed all the joy in her life, and the example that despite her misery she did not capitulate, will hopefully bring stamina to those who struggle with a similar temptation in this closing decade of the century.

A little-known author, Hermann Popert, wrote *Helmut Harringa*, published in Dresden in 1910. His style is pompously dramatic; his idealization of young manhood almost fanatic in exaggeration. The hero, Helmut Harringa, and his close friends are unreal in their strength of character in contrast to the deplorable behavior of the "fraternity brothers" whose misdeeds are recorded in scornful detail. A secret society—unnamed—is formed to rescue the "best" youths from the dangers of hazing and from having to submit to the exaggerated drinking requirements of private clubs or fraternities.

Ironically, the hero's own younger brother, Friedrich, falls prey to the corrupt influence, and after contracting syphilis during a disastrous session of wine and women, he finds himself "compelled" to take his own life. Helmut's reaction is clear: there was no other rational or honorable course for his brother to take, even though the full blame is placed on the irresponsible companions who induced him to join them on the spree.

Another hapless character in the story is forced during a hazing episode to drink himself into a stupor which effectively puts an end to every worthwhile aspect of his life. No longer able to realize his own actions, he is embroiled in a riot, accidentally getting caught in a life-threatening situation from which he saves himself by attacking the mob which corners him. The crowd simply vanishes, leaving him with a murder victim and evidence pointing to him as solely responsible. He is carted off to prison, and comes out of the drunken stupor to find himself (a college student with an expectant and ailing wife who has no one else in the world) certain of at least a long prison sentence.

This, he knows, means his wife can never recover from the shock; she will die and so will the child. His prison term leaves them without any protection. All for one night's involuntary revelry. The reader is allowed to decide whether the final paragraph means he goes completely mad, or decides to make reparation by ending it all.

Long passages of cryptic and almost cultic fantasizing tout the high excellence and noble character of the members of the secret society who, under devoted subservience to a super-leader, will naturally outlive those whom debauchery will have led to their death either through choice or fatal disease.

In some sense, however, the most sinister and disturbing element in the book is the undisguised worship given by the author to the hero, Helmut, who finds an equally superb and perfect mate by the name of Helga; and their son, Hermann, seems to surpass them both. Their virtues and attributes just miss being divine. History knows the mania for a super-race which surfaced in the Hitler era; Edith's sensitive nature must have detected signs of it in her environment and she would have suspected its dangerous potential for evil. In any case, Edith became physically ill as a result of reading the book, and a near-religious experience had to restore peace to her troubled heart. Coming events, especially tragedies, may well cast their shadows into the psyche long before their outlines become clear and recognizable.

Edith made no later reference to the Harringa story but, as we shall see, in 1920, events involving a whole handful of people from the Philosophical Society to which she had belonged, Hans Lipps among them, distressed her so deeply that, once more, she was made ill as a consequence.

Following the development of her spirituality, one can actually see this parallel surface. The circumstances attending her "cure" from each of these illnesses are of the greatest significance. When she was twenty-one, release from the overwhelming burden, which she was unable to shake off herself, came from an exceptional source. She described it in great detail in her *Life in a Jewish Family*. Her spiritual equilibrium was restored at a Bach festival when the chorus sang the Lutheran hymn: "A mighty fortress is our God!" This was during her self-styled atheistic period!

Whether or not she was aware of something like a premonition, Edith in recounting the story truthfully credits a natural rather than religious attitude as the restorative. She recovered peace of heart and mind because she was able to renew and strengthen the confidence she had in her friends and associates. These young people just could not be like those described in the Harringa tale.

At first, Edith's courses at the University of Breslau had

been directed toward the study of psychology, but honesty compelled her to admit her deep attraction to philosophy and she followed its call. Significantly, her mother sensed what this radical change of direction would mean in Edith's life. Frau Stein could not have known that her daughter was taking a first step toward a position which few of their relatives and friends could understand and endorse. Again, it seemed that shadows of events in the future were already appearing on the scene. A foreboding Frau Auguste expressed to her grandchild, Erika, that Edith "no longer loves us and is going away" was mistaken, for Edith never stopped loving her family. It proved true where separation from her loved ones was concerned. Philosophy was, for better or worse, her lodestone and it was to lead her on to Göttingen. The heavy cost of leaving her mother's home to study under Edmund Husserl was accepted honestly as the only way open to her if she wished to be true to herself.

6

Gateway to the Future: Göttingen (1913-1916)

New beginnings have meaning for everyone. And for Edith Stein, April 17, 1913, was a beginning unmatched by any other in her twenty-one years of life. She was embarking on her career as a philosopher by enrolling at the University of Göttingen where Edmund Husserl taught his phenomenology. Göttingen ("where one always and only philosophized, whether one ate or drank, whether one was alone or in company, silent or in conversation") promised to fulfill all her dreams. Her student quarters were comfortable; she had one of her best friends as a congenial roommate, and their youthful landlady made their stay as pleasant as life at home would have been.

Edith was free to select the courses she wished to take, and especially in her chosen field of philosophy she could not have desired more. Her "master", Edmund Husserl, dominated the picture, but he was not as personally important as her other mentor and friend, Adolph Reinach, and his bride, Anna.

Perhaps the deepest source of satisfaction for Edith lay in the brilliance found among her peers. It was a new experience for her to have as partners in a class so many young persons of her own age with such penetrating minds. One senses a kind of exhilaration as she speaks of the intensely engrossing discussions and gatherings she attended. Almost from the first meeting, she joined in the discussions no matter how advanced they were in theme, and how new the topics were to her.

If any of her comments were inept or unfounded, it mattered

little since her companions in the Philosophical Society accepted her participation as a matter of course. Only one feminine member of the society took her readiness to join in as "forward". When Edith became aware of this judgement, characteristically, she admitted her possible lack of due restraint but continued as always to take part in the discussions, both defending and maintaining her personal views. The first few semesters from April, 1913, to June, 1914, were, therefore, all that Edith could have wished them to be. In Breslau, she had been teased for dreaming more about philosophy than about suitors. Now, in Göttingen, the growing interest she took in the personable and brilliant Hans Lipps, and the interest other classmates showed in her, were not allowed to distract her from her main objective of becoming a competent philosopher.

In her account of her relationships in Göttingen, a changed Edith is found. If Hugo Hermsen challenged her to find in the new university town what he charged her with failing to discern in Breslau—persons who met her expectations—Edith seems to have settled that score. But, as we are unable to detect an absolutely radical change in her, it may be that Hermsen's assessment of her was too severe. She had high standards for others because she lived according to those herself.

Should she have to be almost brutally frank with a friend about her faults, as she had been in Breslau with Rose Guttmann, she managed even in that castigation to demonstrate her love so strongly that Rose was happy to go to Göttingen with Edith that first year. Edith's habit of honestly reporting others' complimentary or, just as readily, their negative reactions to herself requires us to note as a backdrop details necessary for a just evaluation of each situation.

The criticism from Hermsen was apparently categorical: you demand the impossible from others. And Edith accepted it, as she says, as a warning. It can serve so in two ways, and it is well not to allow the scales to tip too heavily in Hermsen's favor. He was an influential person in the pedagogical circles of Breslau, and from Edith's mention of him, one automatically assumes that here was a man of high principles and sound judgement, and his cautioning remarks to Edith were for her best interests.

However, to delineate a true portrait of Edith, it should also be mentioned that some of her criticisms probably made Hermsen examine his own actions and attitudes, even though Edith does not mention including him in her censures. Biographical references to him by other authors in that pedagogical group are not flattering. Whether he deserved criticism or the esteem evident in Edith's writings is not of prime importance: what we note is Edith's acceptance of a negative evaluation from him, and her deliberate decision to alter her conduct. She did not stop noticing people's weaknesses. But, far from pointing them out, she now made efforts to keep third parties from becoming aware of them. That is a practical illustration of her dedication to truth, and her acting upon it.

Scholastically, the years in Göttingen were memorable ones for Edith, also. At the completion of five semesters she asked Husserl to assign a thesis to the obvious surprise of the "Master". Somewhat arbitrarily he insisted she clear the decks of possible distractions like her state board examination. She had to review several courses, and at the same time complete her assignment from Husserl on empathy. One gets an impression of her juggling all her activities after her return from the summer vacation in 1913.

Several clues about her manner of working on her assignments, and about her spiritual and physical state are given us for this time. To attain clarity by her effort was an essential; books treating of the matter she was to examine failed to help for the words made no sense, as her mind was actively making its own study of the subject and refused to be weaned from the process. Her mental struggle when writing her dissertations became excruciating for she admits she was unable to sleep and made little effort to eat sensibly; she sacrificed everything, apparently, to the absolute limit of her powers.

Frankly, she confesses she found life almost unbearable at one point. Indeed, her harsh efforts to reason with herself had the unusual effect of compounding her difficulty. At that point, she would have welcomed anything as an end to her misery, "even if it meant being run over on the street, or falling from a cliff on a hike through the mountains."

During this time, Edith gave no thought or allegiance to a God. It was a conscious decision on her part to have nothing to do with a Deity whose existence in her opinion was far from certain.

If one were less sensitive about the painful effect on her physical constitution of this effort to finish her work, it could amuse us to see how on the one hand she ignored God completely while at the same time she admits being influenced by one of her mother's reminders: "As one strives, so will God help" which is the German equivalent of "God helps those who help themselves." No wonder Edith could claim, much later, that her effort to find truth—in her scholastic work at this time—was a search for God.

This was the point in her studies when Hans Lipps' criticism of her work all but paralyzed her. Adolph Reinach, far more experienced than Lipps, and a most able phenomenologist, restored her confidence in her ability to work for clarity. Reinach's appraisal of the thesis made Edith feel "reborn", she said.

That she was suffering is clear from her own account, and that she was alone in coping with it is also clear. Her anguish of heart, brought on by a combination of situations which were all beyond her control, was something she could not discuss with anyone. As a child, she had been without a confidante at home, and as she grew up and found herself away from home, her dependence on her own judgement deepened even though this meant making many painful decisions alone, unsupported by a loving and sympathetic relative or friend. It was a time for learning to lean on God, but Edith was not aware of that, yet.

For these three years, Edith was engrossed in Act III of her life, played with Göttingen as center stage. She progressed with intense concentration and intellectual euphoria through her encounters with Husserl, Reinach, Scheler, and her talented fellow-students, to arrive at a confident expectation of taking her place beside them in the academic scene. Perhaps she would not win star billing but an important role in the supporting cast was within reach, surely.

However, the crashing curtain of World War I cleared not only the stage, but reduced the cast and changed the tenor of the play from dreamy optimism to a realistic view of a future almost robbed of color, reward, and promise.

Edith correctly points out that only those who grew up before the assassination in Sarajevo can have an accurate knowledge of a carefree existence in a world where peace was taken for granted. Since June, 1914, there has not been a time of universal peace—someone, somewhere, has been engaged in "making war". And those who make it most determinedly hardly ever fight personally. Others must do so and risk life and hope. The static complacency, once shattered, could at best be mimicked by brief or longer periods following an armistice, a treaty, a truce, all of which proved too fragile to last.

Fourteen months were all Edith needed to discover a new world for herself. Philosophy would supersede her former scholastic interests and provide a career goal; and friends became as important in her life and dreams as family and relatives had ever been.

One world remained unchanged, at least for several years: her attitude to faith. Gradually, confronted by her fidelity in the pursuit of truth, she was dismayed, no doubt, to discover that her deliberate denial of an Infinite Being had become untenable. She grudgingly faced the realization that like many of her phenomenologist companions, she tended toward acceptance of a Christian philosophy, but consideration of any commitment, even to examining the inclination, was postponed. There was no urgency; it sufficed to have a vague notion of someday doing something about it, but for the present, her studies and her friends were the sun and moon that made life brighter than it had ever been for her before.

June 28, 1914, brought an eclipse. At different stages, her private worlds were demolished and her future greatness rose out of intense personal sorrow and pain.

If this study of Edith Stein were to be strictly biographical it would need to be told with chronological detail. But for the study of her spiritual development, one ignores dates when seeing how converging events in Göttingen affected her professional as well as her private life.

In Breslau, Edith had been among the pioneer women students at that city's university. In Göttingen, she joined an already established small group of talented women who were acknowledged by most professors and male students as competent partners in the academic world, although women were still denied the right to teach, and until that very year, one professor had refused to admit women to his lectures. When war was declared, Edith returned in mid-semester to Breslau. She was shocked that her relatives could speak of the war as something apart from themselves. She, on the other hand, felt herself to be so involved that only her joining the Red Cross nursing corps could satisfy her need to do something for her country. In performing her duties, she once more showed her deepest characteristic, accepting to the limit whatever responsibilities were placed upon her.

At the military hospital in Austria, Edith had her first experience of personally attending the dying. Soldiers, far from their loved ones, dreaded most of all being alone. When Edith returned to Göttingen after her stint at Märisch-Weisskirchen was over, her landlady, perceptive and outspoken as never before, remarked: "Fräulein Stein has seen much in this time; she has changed, too."

Edith resumed her studies; eventually, it was time for her doctoral examination. Now, a second major change impinged on her plans. The Master, Husserl, was called to Freiburg where he was awarded a professorship. Edith therefore had to go to Freiburg, where all her examiners, save Husserl, would be strangers. Despite that, with pride and satisfaction, the Master informed her that on August 3, 1916, the doctorate and the distinction of "summa cum laude" had been awarded her. In his own way, he acknowledged her giftedness by his joyful acceptance of her proffered services as his first assistant. Edith had come to Göttingen to attend Husserl's seminars; she left it again to follow him to Freiburg where she was to embark on a philosophical career as important as teaching. Before we follow her to Freiburg, we must note an experience in Göttingen which had a definite effect on her personal life.

7

When Friends are True

A crisis in Edith's personal life was precipitated by events in Göttingen late in 1920. Although she was in no way personally involved, the situation affected her future; decisions she made at the time determined the course of her life. Unfortunately, she was arrested by the Nazis before she could write in detail about these developments and the reconstruction must be made from references in her letters and from external evidence. Catalyst for this upheaval in her life was a vindictive lawsuit in which several members of the Philosophical Society including Hans Lipps, had roles of accuser or accused.

Edith's correspondence makes mention of "the process" without elaboration. She writes that Lipps is out of favor with Husserl and is ignored by the Master's family. To Fritz Kaufmann, Edith reports from Breslau that she is in the dark about developments. Her sister, Erna, was to marry Hans Biberstein that December, 1920. Edith's account tells how ill she was during those days from exhaustion and from "interior suffering which I had to endure all alone."

Biographers have conjectured, some with presumption, that Edith would have accepted a proposal of marriage from Lipps in 1920. His letters to Kaufmann give many details of his most personal feelings and actions. He often writes about Edith but never mentions marriage. There is no justification for assuming that Edith was "disappointed in love" by Lipps, and that this caused her to choose the life of a religious, eventually.

Undeniably, she *was* disappointed, but not surprised, by the treatment she received from the Göttingen all-male faculty

when she sought a professorship in autumn of 1920. Her work
for Husserl had coincided with the years of World War I and
when the men returned to the university setting, jealousy of
her work was evident. Bearing the brunt of envy is enough to
cause illness.

Her rejection by the university's board (they returned her
application for a professorship and her thesis without even
reading it) together with Lipps' difficulties and his unjust
"banishment" by former friends added to her mental and physical distress. She knew that the widow of Reinach and their
mutual friend, Fritz Kaufmann, were supporting Lipps. Her
relief at that was turned to dismay when Kaufmann misunderstood Edith's sending a letter from Breslau to the plaintiff in
the suit. The whole situation turned into a tragedy of errors.

Edith left Breslau for Göttingen when she was twenty-one
years old. Her whole heart was set on the study of philosophy.
In fact, in discussions with her sister Erna and their mutual
friends, Lilli Platau and Rose Guttmann, the four had exchanged their views on marriage as it would affect their careers.

Of the four, Edith was most convinced she would never
sacrifice a career for marriage. Still, at that same time in her
life, she writes that she dreamed of finding "a great love and a
happy marriage" although many of her relatives and friends,
unaware of her true feelings, considered her "distinctly cool
and unapproachable."

That she should give such an impression is explained else-
where when she recounts that Frau Stein and her daughters
had strict ideas on social standards which were not shared by
too many of their acquaintances. When cousins of theirs,
reaching their twenties, began to live according to a "double
standard" which the Steins refused to accept, the reputation
for being aloof or having a better-than-thou opinion of herself
was attached to Edith, understandably, more than to any of
her sisters. Else was married long since; Rosa was nearly thirty
and had rejected her relatives' efforts at match-making; Frieda's
marriage had ended in divorce; Erna, everyone knew, was
interested only in Hans Biberstein. That people misunderstood
Edith's attitude to marriage did not trouble her. Decisions on
her future life would be made according to her own standards,
not anyone else's.

Her story does not mention suitors, only friends. But when she writes about attending the meetings of the Philosophical Society in Göttingen, soon after her arrival there in 1913, we do get from Edith herself information about Hans Lipps. She tells us he was twenty-three, tall, slim, but powerfully built, handsome, and, compared to many others in that group, kind and considerate toward the less popular ones in the society.

Given all of those qualities, and noting how many talents and interests he had, he had to be attractive in Edith's judgement. He could well be the unidentified young man whom she "liked very much and whom I could imagine as a future life-partner." It would have been premature in her story to give intimate details of their relationship. When she wrote about any of her friends, Edith did not "anticipate" in her book, therefore her comments about Lipps when they met in 1913 cannot be taken as her final, mature evaluation of him. Her letters do show that while she always championed him to her friends and was hurt when the Husserls were harsh and unkind to Lipps, she herself saw his character weaknesses clearly.

In the first months of their acquaintance, Edith was truly fascinated by the versatile young man who got his medical degree that July, at the same time he was enrolled in Husserl's philosophy courses. Additional studies in natural science were his relaxation from the stress of preparing for his preliminary exams in medicine. He was certainly an extraordinary young man, totally unlike anyone she had ever known in Breslau.

She did not talk much about him to friends, and, it seems, even less to her family. Possibly, as the years passed and Edith knew Lipps better, she realized how much their personalities differed, and how they might well be incompatible except as good friends.

When Edith left Husserl's employ in Freiburg in 1918, Lipps was still in the army. Upon his discharge in November, he enlisted on a German mine sweeper to earn tuition for further education. He also took assignments as locum tenens for general practitioners whenever his work schedule permitted.

In the summer of 1921 he was awarded the *venia legendi*, his license to teach at the University of Göttingen. However, he took a year's leave because of financial difficulties, and served that time as ship's doctor on a coastal route from east

Africa to India. His tours of duty on ships were continued into the 1930s; the long vacations from university classes allowed him to sign up for a long cruise every summer.

Edith spent the summer of 1921 at the home of Theo and Hedwig Conrad-Martius helping them in their large orchard, and reading in her leisure. There had to be correspondence between her and Lipps because in letters to Kaufmann, Hans gives news about Edith's whereabouts.

A remarkable hiatus is found in the collection of Edith's letters; none at all to Lipps are extant and only Roman Ingarden kept letters from Edith written in 1921. Perhaps he was the only one to receive any during that year. Kaufmann wrote to Edith in such uncharacteristically harsh terms, late in 1920, that, in reply, Edith says she is now afraid to use words since he misunderstands her so terribly. That letter of hers is deeply moving; it gives insight into her pain but has no reproach for the ones who inflicted it on her.

Despite Kaufmann's exasperation with Edith, his friendship with Hans Lipps was one of the latter's consolations during the lawsuit. Whether Kaufmann felt any jealousy of Lipps whom Edith championed in her letters really is no longer important. Edith's reading of the Life of St. Teresa at the Conrads' home in summer, 1921, made such a deep impression on her that, temporarily, it claimed her full attention.

For some time, beginning after Reinach's death late in 1917, Edith found her self-styled atheism giving way to a growing conviction that she had some kind of belief, after all. The question remained whether, like many of her friends she should become a Lutheran, or whether, like a few others, her destiny was in the Catholic church. The story of Teresa tipped the scales, and Edith became a Catholic on January 1, 1922. Sometime that year, Lipps returned from Africa, and took up residence in the Widow Reinach's house in Göttingen where he began to teach as privatdocent in the winter semester 1922-23.

Edith always pointed out that at the time of her Baptism that New Year's day she received her vocation to the Carmelite Order. She immediately resolved this would be her "profession"; she intended to follow it at the first opportunity, but, to keep such information from reaching her mother in Breslau,

Edith may have kept her resolution in confidence. But she did not dissimulate, of that we may be certain. Her conduct matched her convictions, always.

Hans Lipps married Christine Masing in Göttingen in May, 1923. A daughter, Sabine, was born in 1924; another, Christine, in 1926. Lipps continued the well-paid cruises as ship's doctor every summer. A card to Kaufmann from Cuba tells of being delayed in port there for two weeks but he is not enjoying it and would much rather be with his children instead. Another year, he told Fritz of adapting a summer residence at an inland sea near Munich for his family, and he seemed to spend the short vacations away from teaching at Göttingen with them at Starnberg.

Christine Lipps died of penumonia in Starnberg, July 3, 1932. The little girls were eight and six years old. There is a reference to Lipps as a widower with two small daughters in one of Edith's letters, and she seemed to be informed as the years went by of his moving to other teaching positions. But the references are always brief. Her family had no private information about him, and what may be thought of as a sequel to his wife's death depends on the memory of one person alone.

The account is given by a lifetime woman friend who requested that her name be kept in confidence when recounting her recollection. She said she visited the Stein home often, as she used to study philosophy with Edith in the latter's home visits to Breslau, between 1922 and 1933. The two were reading together one afternoon (not even an approximate date was given for the occasion). Edith suddenly paused as though she had just remembered something she wished to share with her friend and commented on Lipps' being left with the two small daughters. Then she said without more introduction that Hans had recently suggested to Edith that she might "join him and the children."

Surprised by the unusual confidence from the always reticent Edith, the friend could think of nothing more to say than to ask, "What did you tell him?"

The reply from Edith was prompt, and without embellishment, only a couple of words: "Too late." And after those two words, they returned to their discussion on philosophy, and

Edith made no further mention of the incident at any other time, although they kept up a correspondence even after Edith's entry in Carmel.

Some biographies of Edith record a far more dramatic reply: "I told him it is too late, that another had laid His hand on me." There are also differing conjectures about the time when Edith received Lipps' invitation. Her friend's letter gives the wording of Edith's reply, and judging from circumstances would suggest a time between Christine's death in 1932 and Edith's entrance in Carmel on October 14, 1933. What is most significant in respect to Edith's Carmelite vocation, however, is her definite decision to become a daughter of Teresa in January, 1922, seventeen months before Lipps married Christine.

From Carmel, Edith's letters to other mutual friends speak of Lipps, of his teaching in Frankfurt beginning in 1935, and of his being in the military again. In 1939, he was recalled to serve as Army Surgeon at the western border of Germany.

In 1939, also, he married for the second time; his bride, this time, was Catharina Baroness von Welck. In 1940, he took part in a drive on the French front, and then he was transferred on June 22, 1941 to the Russian front. Now, sources familiar with the political situation at the time suggest that his assignment to the eastern front, more dangerous especially if one were taken prisoner, could indicate that he was not in sympathy with the German cause, as it was the custom to assign to that front anyone whose loyalty was in any doubt, or any officer who had objected to other assignments. It seems fully in line with all we know of Lipps, many of whose closest friends and colleagues at the universities were Jewish, to see him remain loyal to them, even if this displeased his military superiors.

On September 10, 1941, he received a fatal head wound at Shabero. He was buried in the military cemetery at Dudino, Russia. Edith received a notice of his death months later, in Holland. She requested prayers for her deceased friend, and could not have known that within months, she too would be killed.

This relationship has been treated at such length because it was one of the most important friendships in Edith's life, one that was bound up with her life decision. Did she recognize in 1920 that Lipps' characteristics did not hold the prospect of a truly successful marriage for her? Putting aside all other obstacles such as her being Jewish, and later becoming a Catholic, her comment about Lipps speaks volumes: "One sees so clearly what he needs, and though one desperately wishes to help him, one knows how impossible that is."

It is certain that the development and the resolution of this friendship was one of the decisive interventions of God in Edith's life. What she learned about herself and about her emotions were things which Edith also characteristically accepted from God's hand. What we learn about her from her subsequent life gives us clues about her handling the matter at the time. She proved, indeed, that once she was someone's friend, she remained faithful to that friendship for a lifetime.

8

On With Life

Superficially seen, Göttingen appeared to offer Edith mostly a mixture of disappointment and chagrin. That is not the case. When any person's story is being told, one episode is taken at a time, but many were being lived conjointly, and what was pleasant in her full days at Göttingen made the difficult bearable, at least, and a challenge to her spirit, at best.

The world was moving swiftly toward a conflagration after which everything would be transformed. When the first World War broke out, classes at the university were cancelled and most of the students and many of the professors exchanged civilian life for that of the military. For half a year, Edith served as a Red Cross volunteer nurse in a hospital at Märisch-Weisskirchen, Austria, caring for German soldiers who had contracted contagious diseases on the Carpathian front. Her mother opposed her decision, but Edith ignored her mother's fear, and followed the dictates of her patriotic attachment to Germany. The six months gave her an intensive course in life and death and made her revise her priorities. Of course, her primary dedication to truth did not need to be changed, but it developed the slow-growing seeds of faith which her studies had sown. She was no longer confident in writing off a Being above and beyond life, although she had very little with which to nurture belief.

When the war was over, and the revolution in Germany brought an end to the time of the Kaisers, there were waves of reaction in all walks of life. Gone forever was the absolute sense of security people had before war spread like the plague to involve the whole world. And in Edith's personal life there was as profound an upheaval. Inexorably, the issue of professional recognition preempted other interests in 1919 and 1920.

It was soon painfully clear that Husserl and his peers in Freiburg and in Göttingen were not ready to admit women to professorship, even in the lesser degree as a privatdocent. Her application was ignored; the thesis she prepared in order to qualify was not even read by the committee which reviewed all applications.

Many of the men she had studied with came back after the war to begin their teaching careers. The medical profession was open to women but university professorships were still reserved for men. For instance, Martin Heidegger was at the beginning of his imposing philosophical career. He was an associate under Husserl when Edith met him at a social gathering at the Husserl home. Heidegger was not always reticent about disagreeing with Husserl, and Edith, then Husserl's assistant, did not hesitate to fence with opponents. Heidegger let it be known he thought of her as "scheming." However, another remark of his gives a delightful image of her which certainly invites a variety of interpretations. According to Heidegger's appraisal Edith Stein knew "who was selling shaving cream!"

Jean Hering, a classmate who became a prominent Protestant theologian-philosopher in Alsace-Lorraine, knew Edith well during her years in Göttingen. He always held her in high esteem "not only for her philosophic ability but for her many admirable traits of character. She had a most tactful way of combining her love for truth with her love of neighbor."

Edith's influence on younger students needs to be mentioned since it was almost a hallmark of hers. One young man, K. Hansen, whose specialty later was research on allergies, wrote to Mother Renata in Cologne to share the memories he had of Edith, whom he met in 1914:

> I was fascinated by Husserl when he addressed the Congress on Psychology in the spring of 1914. I decided to study in Göttingen that summer. [Edith's second year there.] I lived with some people where an older woman student,

[Toni Meyer from Breslau whose story Edith tells in her *Life*.] also rented rooms. This woman was a friend of Edith Stein and the two frequently met in the house. I was 'new' but Edith Stein encouraged me from the start to go to Husserl's class on Kant's 'Critique'. She promised to arrange it. Secondly, she said I should come to Reinach's little private 'colloquies' where he taught practical phenomenological analysis; there I could learn the phenomenological language. Both ventures succeeded.

We met every Tuesday, eight of us in all. Everyone was diligent but also friendly! I told myself often, later, that if I had not had that semester with Husserl, I would not have been able to cope with what I endured at the front.

With Edith and her friends, we often discussed the problem of our attitude to experimental psychology. At first, I was interested in it. Then the discussion would pass on to philosophy and *Wesensschau* (the view of Being). Edith remained a good friend to me; she wrote more than once while I was in action (WW I).

In Freiburg, later, she sent me the dissertation (on empathy) she had finished."

Dr. Hansen had two manuscripts of Edith's which had to do with "Continua." One of them was a talk Edith gave one night at Reinach's. The other was on Husserl's "Ethik." The summer semester had ended in July 1914, and by August, Hansen was in the army. "In 1917, I met Reinach in the foxholes. He was an Observations Officer in the artillery and was temporarily assigned to my battalion. Some weeks later, we were relieved but he stayed there and was killed that year."

Dr. Hansen died in 1963, and the nuns expected to receive the manuscripts he had promised to leave to them, but, unfortunately, they never arrived.

As Edith had been frustrated in every effort to get a teaching position at a university, she began to give independent lessons at home, and had thirty students under instruction. In 1919, she made a repeated attempt to get an appointment in Freiburg.

Edith had been turned down in Göttingen, and the same experience awaited her in Freiburg, and that was enough provocation for her to take some action, even though she realized it would be in vain in her own case. She may have sensed it was a necessary step for *some*one to take or the cause would never go further.

An article published in 1986-7, entitled "Fifty Years of Habilitation of Women in Germany," gives the sequence of interventions in an enlightening way.

A letter Edith sent to Berlin to a man who signed himself simply as Becker initiated a process which took some fifteen years to bear fruit.

> To His Excellency, the Minister for Science, Arts and Public Education:
>
> Esteemed Sir:
>
> Your Excellency will permit me to bring the following case to you for a decision on principle:
> I received the enclosed letter as a decision upon an official application for habilitation at the Philosophical Faculty in Göttingen, in the History-Philosophy Department.
> The exception mentioned in the letter refers to the habilitation of the Mathematician, Frl. Dr. (Emmy) Noether.
> It was repeated to me, orally, that hers was an exception because, in the opinion of the experts who were involved, the lady in question was: "above the average of the ordinary professors."
> The statement was also made that it was important not to make a precedent of her approbation.
> Since there is no justification for this method of procedure according to the conditions regulating habilitation, and, since it is contrary to governmental regulations as well, I am permitting myself to bring the matter to your Excellency's personal attention in the hope that a solution based on principle will be found to this question.
> May I ask, respectfully, that the enclosure be returned to me after you have taken cognizance of it.
>
> > With sincere and deep esteem,
> > I am your Excellency's submissive,
> > Dr. Edith Stein (signed)

The letter she enclosed was from a gentleman named Hermann:

> I regret to inform you that upon consultation with the Pre-Commission, I am not in a position to pass your work on to the Board of Review. Admitting women to habilitation is still a matter meeting with difficulties. The only instance in which it has been done, here, was in an entirely different situation than yours. The officials involved had extraordinary motivation for making that exception. Besides, the woman whom it concerned had extraordinary previous experience; and, in addition, there existed an urgent need for an instructor.
>
> In view of all this, I must beg you to call for your papers and the thesis during my next office hours.
>
> (signed) Hermann

From the Minister of Education in Berlin, Edith received a copy of an interoffice memo, dated February 21, 1920, and it reads in part:

> This decree is from the Prussian Minister for Science, Art, and Public Education and examines, in principle, the admission of women to habilitation. The reply to a contribution received on this subject was sent, according to information received from the Central Archive in Merseburg, to Dr. Edith Stein, at Michaelisstrasse 38, Breslau.
>
> It is therefore assumed that the request for consideration of this matter came from Dr. Edith Stein.

The Minister's message to Edith was encouraging:

> I support the opinion you represent in your communication of 12 December, 1919, that belonging to the female sex may not be seen as any hindrance to obtaining habilitation.
>
> Acting upon this particular case of yours, I have advised

several administrative officials, who handle these matters, of your request.

His notes show that the Education Commissioners at the universities of Frankfurt am Main, Cologne, Berlin, all received copies of the Minister's decision.

Is it surprising to read that some of the faculty were wary of Fräulein Stein? When a correspondent asked her about this complaint, the answer Edith gave fits the picture we have just formed of her. Her return letter says: "The ruling on habilitation sent around to all the universities? I suppose you could say it was evoked by my complaint. But what I did was meant as a rap on the knuckles for the gentlemen in Göttingen."

During the three years leading up to summer, 1921, events and circumstances seemed to multiply, effectively severing every anchoring cord Edith had known since she made her first trip to Göttingen. Several of her best friends and fellow students had died in the war; others who had returned were changed by their experiences, and she herself was no longer the enthusiastic, nearly exuberant disciple of learning. Life's lessons were more formative than the delights study brought to her; a serious attitude to the challenges society posed was her response, and this was noted by acquaintances who remarked that she displayed new qualities they found admirable. Gone was her ready criticism, and in the remaining years it is easy to see how well she kept her vivid critical faculty under the control of a new, warm understanding of human nature.

9

This is the Truth

Authenticity is another word for truth except that it has a nuance of dependence about it. Truth can be thought to stand by itself, and yet that can only be said of God, who is primary Truth. Our individual truths are put to the test at one time or another in our lives. Being brought into God's presence in complete openness, despite our conscious or subconscious efforts to cover-up our shortcomings, is the event that proves our authenticity, our conforming to the Truth which we can only reflect, not duplicate.

A test which proves the image is authentic is often marked with pain. This is due to a deep shake-down; the subject undergoing the test becomes uncertain. In some way, its stability is threatened. The truth that was a firm foundation appears to waver, to dim; and doubt becomes so hostile, or so strong, so real, that there is every likelihood it will take over.

Until it is tested in such a pain-filled manner, the faith placed in truth may be a charade at best and an impostor at worst. Purification of belief may be described in biblical terminology as separating the wheat from the chaff. If these are never separated, the wheat remains true wheat but it is less valuable and presents a risk since one can use it only in limited ways and with unreliable results.

From childhood, Edith Stein showed a fidelity to truthfulness. As she grew older she made contact with more complex and attractive elements of truth. For a while these remained on the natural level, matters which her reason and her common sense could weigh and alter if the need arose. When her friend and mentor, Adolf Reinach, died at war, truth took on spiritual features she had not ever seen before. Her own grief was deep, but, as she travelled from Freiburg to Göttingen as Husserl's emissary, she experienced a helplessness she had never known in all her life. If Reinach's friends were so devastated by his death, how could his widow support her grief? And what could one possibly offer as consolation? Of course, one could help to preserve his memory by having his philosophical work appear in print, but what exchange was that for a beloved presence, for Anna's gentle, "Adole"? How could the widow go on living with her loss?

But upon arrival at Göttingen, Edith found their roles reversed and it was the bereaved widow who comforted her friend; it was Edith whose heart was consoled. Not that Anna was not grieving, but her grief was shot through with hope and a conviction she would someday be reunited with her dearest one. Frau Reinach's courageous acceptance of her loss cast Edith into an ocean of uncertainty. She felt, for the first time, that here a Christian was consistent. Frau Reinach's faith made a difference; her belief in an afterlife gave her strength which no amount of philosophizing could have provided. And it was real enough to be shared with Edith and with all their friends.

Others, Edith's family and friends, observed the manner of her coping with difficult and frustrating situations. First, her work with Husserl failed to give her an opportunity for serious work on her own initiative. Then, after Reinach's death, Edith complied with Anna's request to put his philosophical works in order, again sacrificing time and energy she would have expended on her own research and writing.

Edith's family, seeing her frequently change her schedule to adjust her private life in order to help others, remonstrated, and she was moved to defend her actions in a letter sent to Erna in 1918, protesting that what she did was no more than one would be expected to do. She brushed off their effort to make much of her kindness to others, and her comments on being "saintly", made at a time when she professed to be without belief, are of immense interest since she was numbered among those honored by the title of Blessed in the Catholic

Church, on May 1, 1987. In part her letter to Erna read:

> It seems to me sometimes as though all of you have too
> high an opinion of me and that embarrasses me. For I am
> not at all a saint and have my hours of weakness, just as
> everyone else does.
>
> Besides, I believe that even a saint is not required to
> renounce all wishes and hopes, nor all the joys of the world.
> To the contrary: one is on earth in order to live. One should
> accept with gratitude all the beautiful things which exist.
>
> However, one should not despair if things go other than
> one had expected. When that happens, one ought to think
> of what one still has, and also, that one is only here on a
> visit as it were, that everything which depresses one so
> terribly now will not be all that important at the end; or it
> will have a totally different meaning that we now recognize."

How completely she had internalized her experience with
Anna Reinach! That letter to Erna was written late in 1918,
therefore one may confidently base upon it one's assumptions
about her interior attitude and decision-making in personal
matters which reached their apex by 1920. There are important
reflections in that letter. Her analysis of saintliness is all one
could wish, and conforms, as well, to criteria for happiness,
making a strong point: the two are synonymous.

One can see, easily, that what Edith saw as criteria for
saintliness and happiness are also those which can identify a
true believer in Christ:

> one who has worthy wishes and hopes;
>
> one who accepts with gratitude all the beautiful things
> which exist;
>
> one who also accepts without despair things which go
> awry in unexpected ways;
>
> one who recalls the fleeting nature of life which makes
> passing things unimportant;
>
> one who knows events often turn out to have meaning
> which is hidden at first.

Was it one of those subconscious habits which easily form after one has gained a new insight in relationships that made Edith now look about at the world of Göttingen and Freiburg to weigh her Christian friends' responses to life with renewed expectations?

For more than a year the question remained in the background. She explained to Ingarden during that period that she was unable to see herself "at the service" of any person even though she was willing to do "all manner of things" for anyone out of love. That is a remarkable distinction to make; and Edith even makes it clearer by expressing it as a refusal to "obey" another person. Applying to this her principle of an absolute search for truth, it must indicate that she finds it impossible to believe another will always make trustworthy decisions and demands with which she will be able to co-operate.

There may also be a clue here to her remaining unmarried. Even omitting the promise "to obey" a husband, a commitment in marriage would have implied cherishing and respecting another's philosophy and attitudes toward life, letting go a constant measuring of the other person against one's own yardstick for conduct and belief. Edith had not found the "Master" someone she could follow blindly; Reinach probably qualified, but he did not return from the war. Her younger friends were still away and there was no way of knowing how the dreadful years spent in the trenches would have affected their beliefs and their actions.

For a time she could be optimistic that what she herself experienced was shared by her confreres. That prompted her to propose to her sisters, Erna and Rosa, that they were all living at a time of great change in the evolution of the life of the spirit, meant in a philosophical, not a religious sense. She expected to find everyone more aware, more responsible, perhaps. In her correspondence with Fritz Kaufmann over her philosophical writing she confessed she needed to do more thinking on the problem of the freedom of the will and its spontaneity. By the autumn of 1919, she spoke of having had to open her mental "door" to the philosophy of religion where she must seek answers to some of her questions.

Hardly had peace on the world scene been restored, when

the turmoil of revolution in Germany itself upset the fragile quiet anticipated with such longing. And when some order was restored on the political front, the distressing battle began in the professional circles of Göttingen and Freiburg. This is that "process" already referred to when looking at Edith's progress in her search for truth by December 1920.

Many of the formative events in Edith's life converged to bring her to a point of decision. Breslau and her mother's home had always been there for her. But now, as 1921 was upon them, rest eluded her even in these walls, and, all the more so in the bustling preparations for Erna's marriage to Hans Biberstein. In Göttingen and Freiburg, the lawsuit involving several of her closest acquaintances and the recriminations and accusations against them touched Edith so intensely that her health was affected. She wrote that it was very poor, "probably because of spiritual conflicts" she was enduring in complete secrecy and without any support from family or friends. As she saw the newlyweds off on their honeymoon, Edith decided it was time to "take care of herself" by seriously evaluating her position toward her career and her relationships in Freiburg and in Göttingen. An even deeper conviction surfaced. It was time to reach a decision about her relationship with God. Did she find his existence true, and what difference would it make in her life? Did God make a difference to her acquaintances?

Most of the philosophers in Göttingen who were Christians belonged to the Evangelical Lutheran Church. The Husserls, the Conrad-Martiuses, the Reinachs, or rather, by 1920, the widow, Anna Reinach, were all Lutherans. Hans Lipps' affiliation to a church was never mentioned, but he had been raised by his widowed mother who was also an Evangelical Lutheran. To join a particular church because most of her friends belonged was a choice, but Edith was determined to hold out for her personally essential need, the Truth.

The interior state of her heart, then, as well as the external circumstances in society and world had all come to near-climax. This, of course, is an analysis possible to hindsight, but to see God's operation in the past is as much of a grace as it is to be aware of his intervention while it is happening. To trace the ways of Providence in other lives prepares one to accept and understand how He is shaping one's present for our free response. That is what now took place in Edith's life—now being summer, 1921, which found her once more among the willing helpers at the home of the Conrad-Martiuses in the small town of Bergzabern, where they cultivated orchards. As harvesting was a task requiring willing helpers, the Conrad-Martius home in summer was almost a student hostel, with their young friends from Freiburg and Göttingen welcome as guests and fruit-pickers. The order of the day was practical and simple—during the day everyone shared the chores, in the evening and on into the night, everyone philosophized. Edith spent most of the summer of 1921 at the farm. August brought a short respite of work and Theodore and Hedwig had some business to attend to, so Edith was left on her own for a day or two. Hattie encouraged her to make herself at home, especially, knowing Edith's predilection, in the library.

She herself relates how she stood before the packed shelves and took, at random, a fine thick volume which turned out to be the *Book of my Life* by Teresa of Jesus, the Spanish foundress of the Discalced Carmelite Reform. Edith's further comment is by now, historical: "I could not put the book down and read through to the end. When I closed it, I said to myself: This is the truth."

And this is the statement which allows of several interpretations. Given the line of investigation followed so far in this study, it is taken to mean: "Here, at last, I find a woman of faith who lives that faith in complete fidelity, responding to God, and relating to the Christ in whom she places all her trust in a way that gives testimony to her belief in His Divinity."

In Teresa, Edith found a Christian woman whose lifestyle was consistent with her belief. Teresa was so certain that *her* Master loved her that her belief made an actual difference in her life. Her example led Edith to recognize a "call" to become, first of all, a Catholic and then, a Carmelite nun. From Sacred Scripture we know about a call that woke the youthful Samuel from his sleep. And just as Samuel's response was immediate even when he did not yet understand who was calling and why he was chosen, so Edith responded, at once, in a manner so distinctly her own that her friends remarked upon it. She bought a missal and a catechism the very next morning and began to prepare herself for Baptism. As soon as she was received into the Church, she told her spiritual guide that she wished to become a Discalced Carmelite, a daughter of St. Teresa of Avila. This religious order has a tradition extending back into biblical times. The prophet Elijah is venerated as the proto Carmelite. Of all the Jewish prophets of antiquity, he was the one known for living in constant awareness, in his words: "of the Living God, in whose sight I stand." His challenge to the Jewish people was most logical: "If Yahweh is God, then follow Him."

This kind of testimony to a belief in God is precisely what one observes as Edith Stein's spirituality. Because she believes, every word and deed will in future be in the service of this Divine Master. To Him one can be obedient; in fact, no other course but to obey is conceivable. And a Rule of life which one follows, out of love, will facilitate this loving dependence on God. The life of a Carmelite would enflesh the goal of her search.

Edith's program then, from August, 1921 on, was again a direct one. Study the Catholic faith by means of the most useful books: the missal which contained what she needed to know about the liturgy, and a catechism which was a compendium of the doctrine held by the Church.

When she had studied to her own satisfaction, Edith approached the parish priest in Bergzabern to ask for reception into the Catholic Church. After some additional instruction and a testing of her understanding and resolve, Father Breitling received Edith into the Catholic Church on New Year's Day, 1922.

After that, he was happy to allow Canon Joseph Schwind to direct her in the spiritual life. Honest as always, and aware of the immense truth that, having received Baptism, the one remaining desire she had was to become a Carmelite, Edith informed her spiritual advisor of her conviction that she should enter Carmel. The "call" had come interiorly from God, but it was up to her to make it known to the one would tell her how to go about seeking admission.

And what did Canon Schwind tell her? To make haste slowly, for there were substantial reasons to postpone the thought of religious life in her situation. Religious orders had an unwritten custom, even then, of requiring an interval of at least three years between adult baptism and entrance into religious life.

The first enthusiasm and the intense gratitude converts often feel upon being received into the Church give many of them a pseudo-vocational dream. An adequate return to God for "all He has given unto me", as Scripture puts it, must surely mean becoming a religious.

Gratitude is a key word here. Did not Edith, two years earlier, list accepting all the good things of earth with a thankful heart as a hallmark of "saintliness"? In Teresa of Jesus, Edith met a saint whose gratitude is outstanding in the history of the Church. Teresa claimed and demonstrated beyond doubt that she was grateful for as little as one sardine.

Edith was thirty-one years old when she received the Sacraments of Baptism and the Eucharist in Bergzabern. A short time later, she received Confirmation from the Bishop of Speyer, thereby reaching her "majority" as a Catholic.

She accepted a teaching position at a girls' college run by Dominican nuns in Speyer at Canon Schwind's suggestion, at once giving proof that she sincerely accepted whatever God wanted to give her. Second only to that willingness was her desire to offer to God whatever she could possibly give to Him. It is a clear case of two persons "being in love." Each of the partners sought to outdo the other in presenting gifts, and very soon, Edith again demonstrates a kind of "cunning", plainly the quality which Heidegger misunderstood. (Again, this is an observation of her *modus operandi*, necessary because she spoke so seldom of her spiritual motivation.)

If God loved her so much that his gifts were to keep coming her way every moment of her life, she had one course open to her if she wished to equal Divine Love's generosity. She could make it her life and her love's ambition to give God a receptive heart and mind. Were she to withhold that, even his omnipotence would be unable to present her with tokens of his love.

It seems that friends with whom she had often philosophized expected her to speak of her interior dispositions. But they found a new Edith, one who spoke little about her experience of faith and, if that were possible, even less of her experience of God. To Hattie Conrad-Martius who apparently took for granted Edith's sharing of confidences on their mutual search for God Edith was amazingly abrupt when she replied, in Latin, "Secretum meum mihi"—"my secret to me."

Again, Edith alone could tell us exactly what *she* meant by using this phrase at this particular time. However, the quote is familiar to students of spirituality. It was frequently used to express God's dealings with souls. Clearly, there was no obligation to talk of such personal matters. Teresa of Avila encouraged her daughters to talk together about spiritual subjects in general, but she frowned on making a display out of one's prayer, or "of the secrets of the King."

For years, Edith had known a "Master" with whom she could not discuss her deepest thoughts, whose writings were all she had of his wisdom. Now she could pour out her heart and its most intense yearnings in prayer to her Divine Master for her own needs, and even more, for the needs of the many whom she loved. And during her respectful silence, He replied in His own way. She was not inclined to take time talking to people about God when she could more readily talk to God about people, to their greater benefit at that.

Love, like sunlight, cannot be robbed of its effect. Once Edith absorbed this Divine Energy it seeped out in her speech and in her writing, even in her presence, without effort on her part. She was aware that God made such use of her at times; and she rejoiced in being a channel for his love for those who sought her help. She admitted freely that she never turned anyone aside. This was not a newly acquired trait on her part. She was warm and loving by nature. However, the love she found for and from God transfused itself into the natural stream of caring womanliness for which she was remembered everywhere she went, making it more effective. She advised others to cultivate this generosity as well, recognizing it as a deep source of joy in the Lord.

There is greater misery in our world than the physical hunger taking the lives of so many, more violence than that with which frustrated persons attack one another. The real tragedy is not seeking to know, and the real violence to ourselves not allowing ourselves to believe that God loves each of us completely. Edith accepted it as a fact and the consequences in her life were radical, and simple.

Often, great stress is laid on Edith Stein's "active ministry" in the years immediately following her entrance into the Catholic Church. Some commentators on her life suggest various reasons for the interim between her awareness of a "call to enter Carmel" and her actual acceptance by the nuns in Cologne. Nearly twelve years passed between Edith's Baptism on the Feast of the Circumcision, January 1, 1922, and her admission to the Monastery of the Cologne Carmelites on the eve of the Feast of St. Teresa, October 15, 1933.

Some suggest, for instance, that, since her becoming a Catholic had caused her mother infinite grief, Edith postponed her becoming a nun because such a shock, following upon the first one, would be terrible for Frau Stein. Again, there is speculation that her spiritual guides thought her gifted pen and her lectures would be of greater benefit to the Church than the life of a cloistered nun. Alternatively, others have thought that her director may have questioned the authenticity of the call, coming as so often immediately upon adult reception into the Church, as has already been said.

Whatever the exact circumstances were, during those years Edith reached the summit in her ascent to Truth. She found an effective way to live in continual awareness of God's Presence, a way patterned on the lifestyle she desired but had to postpone. She lived her Carmelite vocation long before she went inside the cloister walls. This is evident in the testimony of those who, without her knowledge, observed her manner of living as a Catholic. It was not a routine, nor did the other Catholic women of her acquaintance have the same habits of prayer, of asceticism, of generosity and of self-forgetfulness which she practiced with unaffected naturalness. There was a very natural reason behind this complete simplicity. As she formerly lived confidently in her mother's home, she was now thoroughly comfortable in her Father's house.

Repeatedly, Edith in her lectures, in her letters, and in her conversations which come after her Baptism, says that she has but a single message to give, that the life of a Christian consists in accepting everything at every moment from the hand of God. This is another way of saying, "If you believe in God, make your actions consistent with your belief. If you love God, trust him."

Everything known about Edith's life once she has become a Catholic has a particular aura about it. Hundreds of persons saw her in her public appearances, and as many more, especially young women, had her as a teacher in the years from 1922 to 1931. Universally, their general recollection of her is as a "woman, praying." Her lectures were memorable, but the principal image preserved of her is not that of a woman active at the podium, or in a classroom. The woman kneeling for hours on a prie-dieu in a corner near the sanctuary of St. Magdalena's, or at a kneeler in Beuron's Benedictine Archabbey, a silent person even known on rare occasions to make an all night vigil in a convent chapel without tiring, this is the Edith Stein whom observers recalled. This is the mystic dimension in her life: she lived her contemplative Carmelite vocation, in anticipation, during her years at Speyer and in Münster.

When Canon Schwind and his successor, Archabbot Walzer of Beuron, both asked her to wait, not three years but four times that long, her acquiescence was clearly in line with her third criterion for a saintly, or mature, person: to be able to accept a change when plans go awry. She could not stop feeling that someday an event completely beyond her intervention or control would make a very big difference in her life, that because of it she would find a treasure which God was "keeping" for her in Carmel.

10

At the Peak: Truth

The higher a mountain, the less likely one is to find people living at the summit, year round, so to say. In the spiritual life that is true, also. But there are exceptions, and one of these "dwellers on the heights" will now demonstrate how she "set up a tent" on the pinnacle of truth once she reached it. Instead of observing any more searching on Edith's part, we begin now to pay attention to the "application" she made in her life of the truth she embraced at Baptism. It is possible to see how she adapted her lifestyle to correspond to her belief in God. She is indeed ready to accept all from his hand.

We come to examine her witness from January 1, 1922, to October 15, 1933, dates which enclose a single endeavor on Edith's part. We look at her, personally. Was there a perceptible difference in her manner toward family and friends? Of course, her visits to Breslau had a new element to them. This is a first indication of the ramifications her Baptism had in her ordinary life.

Edith's niece, Susanne, daughter of Erna, was born in the autumn of 1921. Sue had nine cousins, all older than herself. Her brother, Ernst, was the youngest of Frau Auguste Stein's grandchildren. We learn a great deal about Edith's nephews and nieces from her *Life in a Jewish Family*, predominantly, that between her and each of the children, a very intimate personal, loving relationship was established. Clearly, they could approach her at any time, and expect full care and attention.

Shortly after the beatification of Edith Stein took place, Susanne, now the wife of Alfred Batzdorff, wrote an article about her "Tante Edith" for *Moment* magazine; it appeared in the September 1987 issue. Surprisingly, Sue speaks to her aunt, in a poem, as follows:

> *In that long-ago time,*
> *You kept us at arm's length.*
> *Your time was precious.*
> *You were always writing*
> *Or seeing visitors*
> *We [Ernst and Sue] remained outside*
> *The heavy doors, which*
> *Kept your voices muffled,*
> *Strictly confidential.*

Can this be the same Auntie Edith about whom her nephew, Helmut, said: "When Auntie Edith is here, I don't need you, Mummy"? Did not her tiny niece, Erika, spend hours on the floor beside Edith's desk, looking at books while her doting Aunt was at her work? How explain the change? Erna was Edith's dearest sister, and there could be no question that Erna's children would love Edith as whole-heartedly as had Gerhard, or Wolfgang, Helmut, and Lottie. But about the time Sue and Ernst were born, Edith had become a Catholic. When she visited in Breslau, she went out, quietly, each morning, to the early Mass at St. Michael's Church.

How was she to keep her cherished niece and nephew from seeking her loving attention? They would not have known where she was going, but naturally, they would want to go along. Edith was firmly determined that her own option for religion should not cause a moment of disharmony in her family. The price was high. She had to hold the children, as Sue attests, "at arm's length" to keep them from becoming, like their cousins had been, Aunt Edith's shadows.

One can see from Sue's reminiscences that Edith acted the part to perfection. So well, in fact, that Sue remembers her banishment and, disappointed, protests. Edith's fidelity to the family kept her from complaining about this sacrifice which seems to have escaped their conscious regard.

Neighbors and acquaintances in Breslau would have learned of her conversion and were surely surprised. Some had quite other memories of her from former days when she served as substitute teacher at the Victoria school and had little patience with religious questions. During those earlier years, when Edith was still a self-styled atheist, one young Catholic student of high school age remembered the brush-off, unsweetened in any way, she received from Edith when she tried to give a "Catholic" answer to some questions that arose in class. Edith was consistent; when God did not exist for her, she did not welcome pious talk in class. But after she had herself met God through faith, she learned to allow others to believe or not believe without interference on her part.

We have learned much about Edith from persons who knew her over many years. What may we deduce from the opinions of new acquaintances of hers? She made a deep impression on the renowned Gertrud von le Fort, poet and author of the well-known "Song at the Scaffold." That work inspired Bernanos; his scenario was used for Poulenc's opera, "Dialogue of the Carmelites". The active life and forceful writing of von le Fort and her own entry into the Catholic church as an adult are the background from which she speaks of her friend, Edith. The two met for the first time in 1932, the tenth year of Edith's "public life", those years which distinctly bear a Carmelite seal.

The meeting was arranged by their mutual friend, the Jesuit, Erich Przywara, in 1932. Looking back to that occasion, Gertrude wrote: "We met in Munich, and the meeting left the deepest impression on me: one of great piety, of charming simplicity and modesty joined to a profound spiritual giftedness in this teacher from Münster. My impressions of her were so strong that they had an essential influence on my book, *The Eternal Woman*. During my work on it, I kept calling to mind my picture of Edith Stein which seemed to embody for me what I wished to portray as a "truly Christian woman".

In November of 1934, Gertrud von le Fort visited Edith in the Carmel of Cologne. She evidently was welcomed in the speakroom as a particularly important friend of Sister Benedicta's; the Carmelite had special permission to raise her veil. It was ordinarily lowered, covering the face, during visits from persons other than relatives.

Again, Gertrud recorded her impression: "I saw a face transformed by a look of indescribable joy, which I have never forgotten. Only twice in my lifetime have I seen a human face which overwhelmed me with the conviction that I was seeing a saint: Sister Teresa Benedicta a Cruce and Pope Pius X." (A letter of November 12, 1962.)

In Munich and in Carmel, Gertrude found her impression identical. One might have expected the friend to see Edith somehow "changed" now that she had attained her goal of entering the monastery. Do we discover Edith's secret here? May we call it her "way"?

The heart of this book is surely the place to propose the heart of Edith's "mission" in the Church. By the Lord's providence, we are fortunate to find it described in the language of a mystic. And once more, Father Przywara is to be credited for obtaining such a witness to Edith's relationship with God. During the years when the nuns in Cologne followed up every rumor and hint about Sr. Teresa Benedicta and her sister Rosa, Father Przywara, too, made inquiries and asked his friends to be on the alert for any lead that might uncover reliable testimony about the fate of the Stein sisters.

One of Fr. Przywara's friends was a Swiss Jesuit, Hans Urs von Balthasar, who became known throughout the Church for his erudition as attested to by his writings. Before his death, he was named to the Cardinalate by Pope John Paul II, but in the years of his friendship with Erich Przywara, von Balthasar was perhaps best known for his spiritual direction of Adrienne von Speyr, a mystic whose commentaries on Scripture and whose extraordinary gifts from God are only becoming known.

Adrienne von Speyr shares some similarities with Gertrud von le Fort. Both of them were born into Protestant families; both had established their careers by the time they were received into the Catholic Church. While Gertrud had become known for her literary achievements, Adrienne developed a very large medical practice in Basle, Switzerland. She was instructed in the Catholic faith by the Jesuit von Balthasar, by whom she was baptized. He continued as her spiritual director until her death on September 17, 1967.

Father Przywara's literary work often brought him into

contact with the Swiss theologian, von Balthasar. As a result, sometime in 1946, four years after Edith's arrest, an inquiry from Fr. Przywara prompted his friend to ask Adrienne to describe, if she could, the nature of Edith Stein's prayer. Under obedience, Adrienne gave the following account:

"I see her groping her way along in a prayer of wonderment, which at the beginning appears like a conversation she herself is leading; it is all constructed. It is half-way as though she is asking a question with an idea (of which she is only partially conscious) that perhaps she will not need to be the one to complete the phrase she has begun, nor need she ask the question explicitly, since it may be that God will intervene in the middle of a sentence to make his presence known and to give her question a far more comprehensive reply than she could possible manage, or even expect, to ask for.

And God does actually answer.

Then she prays the more and finally obtains a triumphant certainty at which she is overjoyed.

From that moment of triumphant certainty on, everything is perfectly simple and unequivocal. She will pursue the path God is showing her: she belongs to Him; through love. through faith, she has found again her childlike happiness which has now been augmented and become self-evident.

It would be completely false to assume that her philosophical knowledge helps her to struggle through to faith. The philosophy is incidental. She needs to revise certain things in order to make them fit the faith she has won, but she need not mix matters, nor does she have to prove every definition and formula anew in order somehow to construct a philosophical foundation for her faith.

She is very aware that her faith obliges her to tidy up her faults, to be attentive to a kind of holiness and to awaken it in herself. She has a vague notion of it as an unconditional challenge, not in the sense of a personal mission, but to express her gratitude to God who has called her. She makes the effort, in order somehow to adopt the manners demanded when one is in God's company; in order to permit him to educate her; (she does it) also, in order to make her presence endurable for Him.

She prays a great deal, likes to do so, and becomes constantly more humble and transparent. To renounce the career she has heretofore followed in order to become what God wishes her to be does not amount to a sacrifice for her, not even one in spirit.

Carmel, for her, means obedience and poverty, contemplative life in anonymity, intervening in the Church at the spot where intervention is needed, and, in very great measure, increasing the Church's prayer-treasury. It is (for her) a mode of being in which one thinks only of God, lives only for him, where what is personal allows itself to be obliterated in order to let what belongs to Him become vital and glowing.

In the convent, philosophical work means much less to her than one assumes. It is thrust upon her from outside; she works at it in an obedience which was not of her choosing and which, of herself, she would not have chosen.

And, for her, of course, thinking and writing are done with independence and knowledge, so that they are less difficult for her than other external activities are. Naturally, she hopes that as a result of her work an attentiveness for questions on religion will be awakened in many a thinker. But one cannot say this is her mission. Her mission is that *she prefers* the religious life to the success, the struggles, and the bedlam of the world. External circumstances (in her life), to some extent, distract one from this core of her mission. She was not looking for a refuge in a human sense; it was rather a finding of her final refuge in God, making her ultimate decision for Him alone. Martyrdom, her entering into an even greater anonymity, crowns her mission as she bears the presence of Christ to the extreme place of suffering. However, the principal accent of her mission rests on her entry into Carmel, even more than on her martyrdom.

This appraisal warrants checking against the evidence of her life. In the first paragraph of Adrienne's commentary we find Edith's typical attitude toward God described faithfully. She had earlier practiced the selfsame confident reliance on her mother.

During the vacation before the 1913 Göttingen university semester, Edith had put a question to her mother: "Mama, are you rich?" That was the opener of a conversation which gained for Edith, without her expressing any wish in her own words, the companionship of Rose Guttmann for the first summer at Göttingen. She seemed merely to suggest an idea to her mother. Very soon, Frau Stein herself took the matter in hand, pursued it until she completely understood, and then made all the necessary offers to realize Edith's dream of having Rose with her.

Consistently, we detect Edith's method of actually living her belief in people and in God, even when this was at her personal cost. Her behavior even in incidentals bears witness to her authenticity.

Whenever the topic arose, she informed her listeners that her determination to become a Carmelite coincided with her decision to become a Catholic. That was at the same time equivalent to a statement that she had decided in January, 1922, never to marry. Besides professing belief in the presence of Christ in the Eucharist, she shared Teresa of Jesus' intense devotion to this great sacrament.

As long as she was able to draw up her own daily schedule, she managed to find hours of time to spend in prayer in the Chapel at St. Magdalene's, and later in Münster. This practice seemed a natural consequence to her belief in the Real Presence, and she was so constantly in her habitual place in chapel that her students almost came to overlook her. She was able to surprise them, though, for all that they thought they were familiar with her attitudes and habits. One incident requires some introductory comments.

In her poem about "Tante Edith," Sue Batzdorff gives a word picture of her aunt:

> *Tante Edith has dimples*
> *In her chin.*

Her soft brown hair
Is combed straight back,
A bit too severely.
Are you afraid
To let any wisps
Or curls escape
From the straight and narrow?

To that picture of Edith we add some advice she gave in 1931 to a young friend who was enjoying a busy social life while at the same time entertaining the notion of becoming a religious. Edith frankly tells her that, if her vocation is real, Rose M. is taking big chances with it by expecting it to survive after subjecting it to some strong competition from dating and socializing. Edith claims this credits the vocation with an ability to outlast all the wear and tear to which Rose subjects it. In our European culture there was a proverb, folk wisdom, which applied to a young woman who felt called to the religious life but whose family obligations enforced a waiting period on her. Bluntly, regarding the attitude they were to take to prospective suitors who were unaware of the girl's secret resolve for the convent, the advice was given: "If you are not in the market, don't advertise." In the early 1900s, that did frequently explain severe manners of dress and hair styling.

Edith, as her niece remembers her, had changed in appearance from the stylish young woman depicted in Breslau before her departure for Göttingen in a photograph with her mother, her sisters and their friends. In Speyer, she dressed simply and went about quietly, never calling attention to her presence.

One can imagine, then, the utter surprise of one teen-age student, when one spring morning, she came upon Fräulein Stein emerging from the convent in her best outfit, with hair that had been waved with the aid of a curling iron, and wearing an air of expectancy at once evident in the beaming smile with which she greeted the startled student. Earlier, a reference was made to Edith's response to God as being that of a person "in love", and on this occasion, that state was written all over her. It took a few minutes for the student to realize that Fräulein Stein was on her way to take part in the Corpus Christi procession at the College, an extraordinary, totally unexpected appearance for her in the streets of Speyer.

However, for the ordinarily reticent teacher to publicly join in the procession honoring the Blessed Sacrament was a natural expression of her belief. This was not a "ceremonial" event, it was stark reality for her since she professed her faith in the truth of the Divine Presence in the Eucharist. One may need to be a romantic to appreciate this anecdote as one of the most satisfying of the many reminiscences sent to the Cologne nuns by the women who had known Edith as one of their teachers.

No one ever accused Edith Stein of being disinterested in people. She gave herself tirelessly to her duties as a teacher, even though she would not have elected that profession for her occupation, had she been able to choose. The personal attention she gave to her students' work was at the expense of her own continuing study, or her writing and lecturing, but she cut no corners and gave the young women in her classes the full benefit of her skills and her intelligence. She continued her interest in philosophical matters, however, giving them her careful consideration and writing articles when the marking of papers submitted by her students was finished. Gradually, instead of writing for publication, she was induced to prepare lectures which she gave to teachers' associations, to women's sodalities, at workshops where professional women exchanged views in an ever more serious crisis of education.

Edith's quiet delivery was still forceful. True, some of the listeners complained that she ought to speak louder at a podium, but most of them found attendance at her lectures an unforgettable experience.

The news coverage of her talks in Zurich, Switzerland, for instance, leaves no doubt about her drawing power. Her course of lectures had to be repeated at a second location each time because of standing-room-only available space for each talk. A social gathering followed the lectures, and Edith circulated through the large reception rooms, answering questions and welcoming the opinions of her listeners.

During the course of her years as a lecturer, she exerted a tremendous influence in educational circles in the three German-speaking countries. If she was denied a professorship by the faculties at Göttingen and Freiburg, it seemed God provided her with a much wider audience, and those who heard her were known to credit her with affecting their careers long after her lecturing tours had ended. The contemplative life in Carmel which put an end to her trips to Austria, France and Switzerland, enabled her, instead, to continue her involvement with former hearers through her intense prayers for their work.

Testimonials from students both in Speyer, and in Münster during her years on the faculty of the Pedagogical Institute there, repeat in many forms the same tribute. Edith had a gift for helping anyone who came to her; the teen-age girls at St. Magdalene's, the eager young teachers of Münster, the career women who arranged for or attended her lectures came with a variety of interests and problems. For them all, Edith had a patient ear, and a calm, encouraging word. In her private counseling, the message was the same as the one included in every talk she gave: *learn to live at, and in, God's hand.*

The topics she assigned to her students for compositions reveal her determination to make them act responsibly in their own spheres:

"First weigh the matter, then take a chance."
"Character is the person's destiny."
"I am not a 'cleverly-designed book'; I am a human being with my contradictions."

Personal recollections of her during the years between 1922 and 1933 are individual, but still have a great deal in common. Maria Hatard was about seventeen when she met Edith, "our Fräulein Doktor." Her recollections were sent to Cologne early in the 1960s when Maria was not yet fifty.

She wrote: "We got some idea when we saw Fräulein Stein in Church, of what it meant to bring faith and lifestyle together."

She was quiet, fine-mannered, and calm in class. When she was in charge of our class recreation once each week, she joined in our games. She succeeded in getting permission for us to attend a performance of Shakespeare's Hamlet. We saw it through her eyes as she opened the Englishman's world for us. I mention this because it tells you how great and how open she was.

"I hope she becomes a 'light' so that many can believe God

is visible in people in *our* day."

From sometimes unexpected sources, there were comments about Edith's recollection in prayer. One young boy served the Dominican nuns as altar boy for a number of years. He recalled that after he noticed Edith at prayer, on her prie-dieu in the corner of the chapel at St. Magdalene's he looked forward to his assignments just to see if he could ever notice a change in her manner. Though he observed her for years, his memories were consistent. It was as though no one else were present but Fräulein Stein and the Lord to whom her prayer was addressed.

The reports are amusing, too, as in the case of a young religious at St. Lioba's convent who noticed Edith during the latter's visit in Freiburg one time. Fräulein Stein was so absorbed in her prayer during Vespers that she, the Sister, was totally distracted watching Edith!

Edith put in years of public activity as a Catholic professional woman, lecturing in Germany, Switzerland, and Austria to large audiences of educators and professional women's societies. The foundation of this activity was largely hidden from her audiences, that contemplative, yes, Carmelite, life she lived even in Speyer, Münster and wherever she found herself.

True, not all the comments about Edith at that time were kind or complimentary. Some thought her recollection was an affectation, that her oblivion could not be real, and the length of time she spent in the chapel seemed to them exaggerated, and it made them, somehow, uneasy. This kind of evaluation is important, for it is proof that at St. Magdalene's human nature was alive and well. If, outside the chapel, Fräulein Stein seemed to these same persons so "normal" and their years of observation disappointed their hope of seeing her "drop her guard", the testimony is more trustworthy than if everyone had been in awe of her at all times.

Edith's frugality at meals, and her simplicity of dress also irritated some people in Speyer. But others had first hand experience of another aspect to this lifestyle. One fellow teacher mentioned to Fräulein Stein in passing that there were people in a neighboring village who had been especially unfortunate with crops, or whatever source of income they had. She knew only that they were finding the hard winter especially difficult.

Less than an hour later, Edith came to the teacher's room with her arms filled with winter clothing "for the people in that village." No amount of argument could make Fräulein Stein see that the comment had not been meant as a plea for help. These were things she really did not need, and if they would be of any use during that winter, they should go promptly to those who had use for them.

From a letter written years later in Carmel, we learn of another way in which Edith came to the assistance of someone in an emergency. This time it was her good friend, Theodor Conrad, husband of Hattie, and owner of the orchard where Edith helped to harvest fruit each summer. Evidently, the crop had failed and other expenses had made difficulties, for Edith helped Theo with a loan which she pressed on him with the assurance that it was money she really had no need for. "I'm not allowed to help much at home, even though things are increasingly difficult for the family. So you will be doing me a favor by permitting me to give a little lift at this time."

When Edith referred to the loan again, the Conrad-Martiuses had probably sold the fruit farm, and Theo wished to repay her. Edith told him he could send the money to the Cologne Carmel since, as a religious, she no longer had need for it nor would she be able to make use of it. And, if it could still help him and Hattie, Edith added, he was to recall her condition when she gave it: it was to be theirs for as long as they had use for it, even if it were never to be repaid. So quietly did she give her alms, and help her friends, that for years no one was aware of her generosity. Only the grateful letters after her death showed how many benefitted from her unobtrusive charity.

No doubt, there will be some objections made that her work, her writings in these important years should be brought into this study. But there is always a risk that, once a glimpse is given of her extraordinary intelligence, there will be so much to say on that score that, just as in her lifetime, it will seem to outshine her spirituality, her "secret", which has prime importance for us.

The years at Speyer, nine in all, were as happy as they could be when the horizon kept darkening with Hitler's growing power. The increasing restrictions laid on Catholic educators, and the harassment of anyone who failed to join forces with the Nazis was not lost on Edith. Her experience was double-edged, and she saw all too clearly what too many simply could not believe. What was already unbelievably unjust would only escalate. There are three anecdotes told about Edith which clearly indicate what the 1930s meant for her, and for her dearest relatives and friends: increasing danger.

There were, as one might expect, persons who were fans of Hitler even among the students at the Pedagogical Institute in Münster. One young teacher brought her copy of Hitler's *Mein Kampf* to the cafeteria to read at meals, and she claimed it was the literary gem of a century.

Usually, her enthusiasm was tolerated by the other students who felt it best to let her talk to the air. With the others, Fräulein Stein had put up with a great deal of this young woman's needling, and finally had her fill.When the young lady held forth again on the greatness of the Nazi ideal, especially of women, Edith quietly but in very definite terms suggested the student was far from embodying that ideal, herself, since her chain-smoking would have won her Hitler's deep displeasure. The angry recipient of the criticism was silenced to the delight of the rest of the diners. Edith wondered later whether her remarks had been malicious, but her friends were quick to reassure her they had been only too well deserved.

Well enough to give a piece of one's mind to a student, it might be objected. Edith was not a respecter of persons when it was a matter of frankness. Among the ranks of Catholic professionals there were also discussions of the ever-increasing signs of Jewish persecution by the government. Once, during such a discussion, one man spoke eloquently of the anti-Semitism he deplored, and he was pointing out the injustice of it, when he made a rueful comment that, of course, he had to admit that he knew of one handful of undesirable—but as he was about to conclude the phrase, Fräulein Stein who was usually so quiet and undemonstrative cried out "You must not say it! Today, one may not even *say* such things!"

She was so deeply moved that she emphasized her protest by striking the table with her fist. It was true, things had become so serious that even a lightly meant comment seemed to be a favorable judgement of Hitler's fanaticism. Just so, later, when the nuns in the Carmel of Cologne were expressing the futility of voting since they were convinced the elections were rigged, Edith again showed strong agitation, insisting that one *had* to take every opportunity to show one's opposition, or risk complicity through silence. In Holland, Edith used one of the last opportunities she had to show her determined opposition to a tyrannical order. She said "Praised be Jesus Christ!" every time she should have used the Hitler salute according to law. Not the harshest reprimand of a Nazi official could make her relent, and in the face of her attitude of compliance with what she considered just regulations even from occupation forces, this defiance of Hitler's supremacy must be noted. There will be occasion to examine her obedience to civic regulations later. Here, now, it seemed necessary to point out her disregard of personal safety, and her overcoming her ordinary reticent way, when her sense of injustice was offended. Always, she proved herself true to her convictions.

The third incident is recorded by Edith herself. It happened during Lent of 1933, a few weeks before she was deprived of her right to teach. There had been an evening meeting of the Academic Union attended by most of the faculty of the Pedagogical Institute. Edith returned, alone, to the Marianum where she had a room in one wing of the convent. Several students also had rooms in the same wing but they had gone home for the Easter vacation. Edith found herself locked out and could rouse no one to open the door for her. She had either forgotten her key, or someone had left a key in the lock from inside. In any case, she would have been stranded for the night had not a gentleman passing by noticed her difficulty.

When he offered assistance, he recognized her and within minutes, he and his wife who accompanied him, invited Edith to spend the night as a guest in their home. She accepted with gratitude and accompanied them to the house. While her room was being prepared, the teacher who knew Edith because he, too, was employed at the Institute began to speak of the political situation which was becoming more and more depressing. He was unaware that Edith was Jewish, and in similar cases she always acquainted people with the fact. But, with evident distress, he had just mentioned that American newspapers were accusing Hitler of taking atrocious measures against the Jews, and clearly he wanted to believe the unofficial reports could not be true. Edith felt that he would find no rest that night if, on top of his tale, she were to tell him that she was one of the Nazi targets, so she remained silent on the subject.

From that episode on, she says, there was no longer any doubt in her mind about her own destiny. And, once more, it was a case of accepting from the hand of God, much like the biblical Job, whatever was offered. If the demonic ill will of human persecutors was preparing the worst for her, she would place her trust in God's ability to come to her aid with strength for whatever lay ahead. She believed that God would be with her as he was with the three young men when they were cast into the fiery furnace by another tyrant. In God's hand she would take refuge, come what may.

What came, first, was an answer to her longing for admission to Carmel. By April 1933, the Nazis were systematically cutting the ground out from under the Jewish community, and teaching, writing, in fact, any professional or business career, were all prohibited to those of Jewish ancestry. There was no prohibition against entering religious congregations, but this was not an indication of tolerance. The Nazi plan would take care of *all* religious eventually, so for the present, unless their houses or property were already tempting to Nazi greed, there was no interference on that score. The religious were expected to know that accepting anyone with Jewish blood would have to be "paid for" and this was thought to be deterrent enough.

Edith requested permission from her spiritual director, Archabbot Walzer, to apply for admission at the Carmelite monastery in Cologne. She had just received her dismissal from the Pedagogical Institute in Münster, and the time had come when her hope of Carmel was to be realized after eleven years of patient waiting. The abbot gave his consent, and in a remarkably short time, Edith received confirmation from the nuns in Cologne that her application was approved by the Community. With that, we arrive at the final stage of her living the truth—this time, her vocation to the contemplative Carmelite life.

Part of the joy awaiting her in the monastery at Cologne was the realization that her life had truly "come together" in that her contemplative hours now became her prime "activity". This would surely be the *moment of triumphant certainty* referred to by Adrienne von Speyr. Edith would finally be able to live within a monastery the prayer life that had sustained her during her hours in a classroom, in a train bound for Vienna or Paris, in her mother's kitchen, or in a Zurich lecture hall. At that time she had no idea that this same prayer would sustain her as well in Westerbork and Auschwitz. We know it because at every step along the way, Edith Stein was faithful to her lodestar of truth, and her code of personal conduct never changed.

11

The Night that was Light as Day

We have seen how St. Teresa's account of her personal response to Jesus Christ, and of her intimate knowledge of him whom *she* called "Master" resonated in Edith's mind and heart.

During her years as a student or a fledgling philosopher, Edith had considered Edmund Husserl, Adolph Reinach, and in a more limited degree, Max Scheler and other professors, as guides in her professional life. She always spoke of Husserl, simply, as "the Master. It required just such an astute understanding as Edith possessed to see in the relationship between Christ and Teresa of Jesus a prototype, in a sense, of the interaction Edith had known with her mentors in Göttingen and Freiburg. It was possible, then, although this had not occurred to her before, to establish an even more dynamic relationship with Christ than she had enjoyed with her "Master" in phenomenology. This was indeed a measure of truth to satisfy her to the full at last.

In none of her letters or lectures do we find a detailed explanation of the exact meaning of her conviction as she closed Teresa's *Book of her Life*: "That is the truth. But we may be sure she did not merely discover it, and then discard the notion. She definitely acted on it.

For her, as for the biblical Samuel and the prophets, God was so great that she knew it was fitting for some persons to offer their lives exclusively to him in gratitude and praise. Her deepest hopes could be fulfilled by such a life; it held challenges unequaled in the secular sphere, even though it appeared as darkest night to relatives and friends who could not understand in faith.

The life of a Discalced Carmelite nun, modelled on the life of Teresa, was for Edith a career as demanding as any professorship would have been, even though there was much less external activity to attest to its demands or its success. She would allow herself to learn about the life of a Carmelite nun in the same way anyone else who entered the community in Cologne-Lindenthal learned, by living it.

Once her application was approved, Edith was invited to spend some weeks in the "extern" quarters, the guest rooms outside the enclosure of the monastery. Here she could follow the daily schedule, or horarium, of the community and get some feel of the even tenor of their lives even before her entry into the cloister. However, interacting with the prioress, with the mistress of novices who directed newcomers, and with the other Sisters remained to be learned.

Assimilation into the community is a gradual process, and perhaps too much was taken for granted about a newcomer's ability to grasp intangibles. In Edith's case, however, one may be certain that she saw how things were done in the community. It is just as certain that, with her wide experience and her understanding of human nature, she saw the human limitations of the nuns, be they her peers in the novitiate, or even the superiors of the Community. This certainty guarantees that in her Carmelite life, Edith Stein found both a challenge to her faith and love, and full satisfaction in her search for truth in the Carmel of Cologne.

In 1933, as for many years before and at least another twenty-five years later, a candidate in Carmel spent at least six months as a *postulant*. The word designates "one who asks" to be accepted by the community. Although postulants as a rule dressed in a black uniform unlike the Carmelite habit, they followed the daily schedule of the community. They, too, were bound to keep the law of enclosure. Unfamiliarity with religious orders has given some persons reason to speculate whether women who choose a cloistered contemplative life have valid motivation for so different a lifestyle.

Are they free to enter, or have they been talked into it, or even tricked in some way? Once they have entered a monastery is it possible for anyone to leave if they find they have been mistaken about a vocation? For Edith, freedom of choice, freedom to leave at anytime, and freedom from coercion, inside or outside the cloister, were all ensured by the Nuns' Constitutions which governed the Order when she was admitted in October 1933.

These Constitutions decreed that a woman be admitted to the Community only after the postulancy during which time she is under no obligation to stay, and there are no conditions to be met before she can return to the secular life, if this is her wish. Likewise, should the Community, during the months of postulancy, have serious reason to feel the applicant does not possess the health, temperament, faith conviction, or adaptability to community life which augur for her happiness and satisfaction in the Carmelite life, the nuns may suggest to the applicant that a reassessment of the vocation should be made. St. Teresa was clear on this subject: a discontented nun and a sad saint were not her choice as daughters in her monasteries.

After completion of the postulancy, the aspiring Carmelite is received into the Novitiate. Again, the Constitutions in No. 231 provided criteria: the novitiate is valid when the conditions of canon law regulating the incorporation of members are fulfilled. There are provisions made to protect anyone from being coerced: admission is declared invalid if a person entered under the influence of compulsion, grave fear, or fraud. The community is also given protection: the admission is invalid if the superior received the person under pressure of any of these same negative influences.

Anyone burdened with debts and with no way of paying them; children whose duty it was to take care of dependent parents or grandparents; or, on the other hand, parents who had children still requiring parental support, guidance or education, all these were refused acceptance. These impediments make clear that admission to the religious life is granted responsibly. It would be very difficult for anyone to enter Carmel merely to escape some duty or situation which had become onerous.

Edith Stein's mother grieved sorely at her daughter's decision; had Edith been an only child and her mother dependent on her in her old age, the story would indeed have had a different plot.

With all of this basic information on life in Carmel, can we see what there was "to" it for Edith Stein, personally?

12

I Will Lead Her to the Desert

Put on the breastplate of justice, that you may love the Lord your God with your whole heart, and with your whole soul, and with your whole strength, and your neighbor as yourself. In all things take the shield of Faith, wherewith you may be able to extinguish all the fiery darts of the most wicked one, for without Faith it is impossible to please God.

Excerpt from *Primitive Rule of the Order of the most Blessed Virgin Mary of Mount Carmel.*

History textbooks, dictionaries and encyclopedias, as well as biographies of men and women who spent at least part of their lives in a religious congregation, mention the existence in that culture of something named "the Rule," but an explicit quote from one or other of these most venerable of all 'how-to' manuals is seldom given. Edith Stein discontinued a lifestyle familiar to her relatives and colleagues and so to say vanished into a world unknown to them. The perplexity of those who have no notion of how a day, much less a lifetime, could possibly be spent in a monastery deserves to be dispelled. By obtaining as realistic a picture of that life as Edith gave of her years in the heart of her family, in Breslau, and among her friends and associates, one gains insight into her "interior" life which was "in the Lord," enabling us to learn her ways.

The family unit into which the tiny Edith had been born had its own individuality, and its goals were clearly definable. Had anyone taken the time to write out the parents' determination to provide proper housing, clothing, and education for their children, along with whatever else might ensure for all a happy, wholesome family life it would have been a most matter-of-fact equivalent of a religious rule. The Order (Carmel, in this case) is a family which regulates how one may recognize its members. They will be known as doing such and so. This one will be the head of the family, for such a time. And so on.

Years, nearly five, elapse from the time a woman is received into a community of Discalced Carmelites until she becomes a permanent member of this household and family. The Rule followed by the Carmelites is their strongest bond to the very land from where the first hermits migrated to the west of Europe after the time of the Crusades.

The Rule, given to the hermits on Mount Carmel in Palestine contained the exhortation quoted fully above. The heart of their life is enshrined in the single sentence:

> Love the Lord your God with your whole heart, and with your whole soul, and with your whole mind.

Another source, even more venerable than the Carmelite Rule, had made Edith Stein familiar with this injunction from her earliest youth. The Shema of Israel was dear to Frau Auguste Stein and there was surely a fervent moment of loving remembrance of her mother every Friday of her nine years in Carmel when the Rule was read aloud to the Community, and these words echoed in Edith's ears and heart. She was not yet aware that this most honored phrase had been incorporated in the Rule when, in Breslau, on the morning of her forty-second birthday, Edith accompanied her eighty-four year old mother to the synagogue because it was the last day of the Feast of Booths.

On the long walk home, Frau Stein brought up a topic that had already been exhausted in their many discussions. It seemed a final, urgent effort at least to understand what her youngest daughter could mean by becoming a nun. "God is

One, Edith, did you not hear: the God you are to love is *one*?"

In silence, both women knew that they loved that God with wholeness of heart, soul and mind. But of the two, Edith alone felt that it was the *same, one God* they both believed in and worshipped.

There was no turning back from her resolution. Edith was too much like Auguste to be distracted from her vision of the true course for her.When Siegfried Stein died, Auguste's relatives had been convinced that her happiness and the well-being of her children demanded the sale of the lumberyard and a livelihood as owner of a boarding-house for the forty-four year old widow. Edith, a mere two years younger when her teaching career was wiped out by the Nazis, did not justify her own determination by citing her mother's courageous example, but it is not surprising to us that she did not reverse her decision even at the sight of her mother's anguish.

Frequently, to the sorrow of those who love most deeply, it happens that, for some principle, they cause almost unbearable pain to a cherished relative or friend as though such deep love could be had only at exorbitant cost to all involved. This was one sorrow which mother and daughter experienced in a shattering new dimension: instead of being halved by the mutual bearing, it seemed to be doubled and redoubled to an infinity of pain. The walk home from the synagogue was finally concluded in a silence which showed how deep was their mutual respect for one another and for the other's sorrow.

The rest of that October 12, 1933, was spent in a family celebration of Edith's birthday. All her sisters and brothers were relieved that the gathering was other than an outward farewell. The only mention of the impending separation was made between Edith and Erna. Else and Rosa were to accompany Edith to the station for her early departure on the 13th. Erna was to remain at home with their mother since she would be best able to comfort the distraught matriarch.

No one at Michaelisstrasse 38 slept soundly that night, and only Edith rose early. She went as usual to morning Mass at St. Michael's Church. The archangel was patron of the neighborhood; Edith was comforted at the thought of leaving her loved ones in his watchful care. They had lived on the street named in his honor for many years. Edith's large, comfortable workroom-studio was now cleared of all her books and papers. Had she gone only on a speaking tour, they would have been left undisturbed. Now, they were packed into boxes for forwarding to the monastery in Cologne since her relatives scarcely had an interest in them. This was a most eloquent symbol that Edith was leaving permanently, this time.

Early, then, on October 13, three women waited at the Breslau station for a train that was late, as though it had sympathy for the eldest of the trio.Else Gordon did not want Edith to leave; she clung to her until the last moment. When Edith boarded the train upon its eventual arrival, Else's grief was so apparent that Edith was shocked; Else suddenly looked old. Rosa, on the contrary, was quiet, but happy for Edith and silently saluted her.

This sister was the only one in the family who had come to share Edith's belief in Christ. Had it not been for their mother's advanced age, Rosa would also have become a Catholic, but, out of love for Frau Stein, she continued to take care of the household and was her mother's constant companion in the home. Rosa understood Edith's call to Carmel only too well: it would have been her greatest joy to go along. Instead, she stood with Else, waving kerchiefs until the train was out of sight.

Edith was on her way to an entirely new way of life. For what might well be the last time, the beauty of Silesia passed before her eyes. October was a glorious month, and the train rushed on as though anxious to show her everything at once: acres of wheat, barley, oats, and flax, fields where potatoes and beet crops had just been harvested; and, off in the distance, the mountains; closer, hills with ruins and regal castles on their heights.

In cheerful contrast, the huge farmhouses, in bucolic humor, had whole verses painted on the facade to invite the passerby's admiration or skepticism. How often on their hikes in the Riesengebirge had Edith and her friends laughed at those verses! How well one artist's work emblazoned on a barnlike home expresses what Edith felt on that day.

> Three months of summer, nine of snow
> One God, one roof, two geese hold sway.

Home means so much, our folks all know
We're like to die when we move away.

Now, were Edith, in moving away, to find her desires fulfilled,
what of the cost to her mother, her sisters?

There had been friends and relatives who suggested that
Frau Stein might not be able to sustain this grief, not actually
putting it into words, but clearly implying that Edith would be
responsible were her mother to pine away. This, too, had to be
accepted, and placed into God's hand. For His sake, Edith
was willing to relinquish the care of her dearest ones to God;
she would look forward to what lay ahead, not in stoic indif-
ference to their pain but in faith and hope. Still, her mother's
tear-streaked face kept coming to block out the scenes flying
by outside the window of her compartment. Edith decided to
write some farewell notes to her close friends to whose prayers
she commended her mother; she would at least do what she
could to ease her mother's sorrow.

Late that day, the train arrived in Cologne where she was
met by Herr and Frau Spiegel-Hess. Hedwig Spiegel, Edith's
god-child, had begged her to be their guest for this last night
before Carmel welcomed her within its cloister. Whether these
friends themselves understood what it would mean in actuality,
Edith could not know. To someone who had not the call to
Carmel, the rule seemed almost implacably hard. Like many
cultural circumstances which have been radically changed since
the 1940s the observance of cloister in contemplative monasteries has been adapted according to the directives of Vatican
Council II. To get a vivid image of the real upheaval in the
lifestyle of Edith Stein as it affected her contact with her
friends and relatives it is good to document what the prescriptions called for in that year. To quote from the rule which
Edith observed has a single purpose, to eliminate any uncertainty as to exactly how she was asked to live in her community.

There are legends and suppositions in abundance about
Carmel and its customs and practices. Many of the observances
of the life in our monasteries during the 16th to the 20th
centuries have become familiar to readers of Teresa of Jesus,
John of the Cross, Thérèse of Lisieux, and Elizabeth of the

Trinity. But the literal prescriptions of the Rule are not always known, and it is well to see them, remembering at all times that this Rule which is a living "organism" has to be expressed in a living way in Spain, in Australia, in the Netherlands or in Hawaii, wherever Discalced Carmelite nuns have taken the Rule and Constitutions.

We have seen that the Carmel of Cologne was the first monastery in Germany, founded in 1637. The cornerstone of the monastery where, today, the memory of Edith Stein brings together persons from all over the world, was laid in 1643. The very location of the church which Sister Benedicta visited as she left for Holland on the eve of the New Year, 1939, is held sacred in the Church's memory as "Martin's field". Here, reputedly, St. Severin, Bishop of Cologne in 397, saw in a vision his friend and colleague, Martin, Bishop of Tours, being conducted into the heavens by angels—receiving in this way the news of his friend's death. Edith has a share in an ancient heritage, indeed.

What shall be made of one fascinating coincidence found in the interior of that church, built in 1642? To decorate the ceiling directly above the main altar, the architect, an unnamed Carmelite lay-brother, at the suggestion of the highly artistic prioress of the Community, Isabella of the Holy Spirit, designed a six-pointed star—as many points as there are in the star of David. Three-hundred-and-fifty years later the picture of Blessed Sister Teresa Benedicta of the Cross, Edith Stein, was hung below that star and it is there that her memory will be recalled with love by the religious descendants of those first Carmelites of Germany.

If the very building contains a symbolic reference to Blessed Edith, its history as well shows parallels of harsh treatment on the part of the German government. In the first secularization of 1802, the nuns were evicted from the monastery when all church property was confiscated, and on July 4, 1802, the sixteen Sisters in the community took shelter in a private home offered to them as a refuge. There deprived of the privilege of living publicly as a community of religious, and forbidden to accept new members they continued to live according to the rule as best they could. The last member of the group died there on February 17, 1842; eight years later, the Carmel was refounded, but only for a quarter of a century. In 1875, when extreme measures were taken by Bismarck against religious orders in Germany, the nuns chose exile in Holland in preference to secularization. Only in 1986 were they able to return to make a third start as Carmel in Cologne. Now, for nearly half a century, despite the deprivations of World War I, the community grew and lived peacefully in Cologne-Lindenthal. They often thought with love and longing of the building that was the cradle of Carmel in Germany; would they ever be in a position to reclaim it?

The ravages of the Second World War left their mark on the Martin's field section of Cologne. A thousand hours of bombings—they began soon after Edith left for Holland and continued until 1945—did not spare the venerable parish church. That interior in which Sr. Benedicta knelt for a farewell visit on December 31, 1938, was gutted although the walls and the ceiling with its David's star withstood the fire.

Allied bombs completely destroyed the monastery in which Edith had lived, in another sector of the city. When hostilities ceased, by the goodness of Divine Providence, through the intervention of the Archbishop of Cologne, Cardinal Frings, the nuns were invited to return to their original location. The charred interior of the Church was restored. It became the first ecclesiastical structure in the Martin's field sector to be opened for public worship after World War II. The work of restoration took ten years and had the support not only of Cardinal Frings but also of the Lord Mayor of Cologne, Konrad Adenauer, who served a few years later as Chancellor of the *Bundesrepublic.*

This is the historical setting for the community that became Edith's religious family on October 14, 1933.

13

A Door Opens

The religious may not be seen without veil except by their parents, brothers and sisters, or in some other case where there may be an equally just reason, such as for some necessary or reasonable cause, but then only by such persons as may be likely to help the religious in the practice of prayer and give them spiritual consolation rather than recreation.

On the Enclosure. From the Constitutions of the Discalced
Carmelite Nuns. Issued January, 1928.

When Edith Stein became a postulant in the monastery at Cologne, these were the regulations for the "enclosure of the nuns". Since her time, after Vatican Council II, adaptations in line with the renewal of religious life have been made, but there are still provisions for enclosure. When their true function is considered, such provisions are both reasonable and pragmatic. They are positive measures taken to provide the conditions most conducive to a life of prayer.

What is avoided is unnecessary or superficial distraction. Contemplative prayer excludes no person or need; access to it is free and available to everyone, be they an old acquaintance or a stranger. Monasteries receive calls constantly from persons carrying burdens of illness, unemployment, family problems, or other concerns, who wish to enlist the support of the religious. Such requests never "break" enclosure. There are members of the community to accept calls and visitors; the intentions, however, are remembered by all. The silent recollection, the concentration, of the individual members is not disturbed, and this is what "enclosure" is meant to provide.

More evident as "enclosure" is the provision that contemplative religious attend few outside activities; they are said "seldom to leave the enclosure."

For Edith Stein, this was the more serious stipulation, and it was the one her family found difficult to understand for it seemed unreasonable. Edith's mother was too old for a journey from Breslau to Cologne; if Edith were never allowed a home visit, that meant she would never be seen again by Frau Stein. Therefore, on October 14, 1933, as Edith and her friends came to the monastery to attend Vespers in the afternoon, she was making a definitive break with her family as well as with the world she had known.

The ceremony at the time of her entry after Vespers on the eve of the Feast of Saint Teresa was simple but expressive, as suggested in the books of customs used in Carmelite monasteries for centuries, in all parts of the world:

> On the day fixed for her entrance, the Prioress and Council receive her at the enclosure door. They do not raise their veils until the door is closed. The postulant kneels; the Prioress presents the Cruxifix to her for her to kiss and gives her the blessing. Afterwards, her Reverence and the other Sisters present embrace her. She is then conducted to the Choir to make a visit to the Blessed Sacrament and to offer her sacrifice to God. She kneels a moment at the altar where our Blessed Lady is honored. Then, she is taken to the recreation room where the Community is assembled. The Mistress of Novices leads her around to embrace the Sisters, and after a while she is taken to the cell prepared for her.
>
> -Excerpt from the Book of Customs for our Nuns.

In this way, Edith's Carmelite life began officially. Her family and friends might and did visit or write but a line of demarcation was set.

However, by being accepted into the Cologne community, Edith gained a new family of sisters. Now, for a time, she was once more the youngest, and therefore entitled to special attention, cooperation, and loving help from her older sisters. And for the first time since her reception of Baptism, she was a religious among other religious who had the same hunger and need for silence and prayer she had always shown in Speyer and in Münster. In return for these gifts from her new sisters, she had much to offer. The talents and giftedness she brought would enrich the group; her interrelations with these new sisters would express her own spiritual attitude.

A strong personality is required to live in Carmel, and strength builds on intelligence. The principal role for the mind in the contemplative life is that of listener, and that explains the need for silence and freedom from external stimulation of a social nature. To listen to God who speaks within, one has to forego conversation exteriorly, and to be silent, interiorly. To respond to God, after listening to him, is to pray. The Rule of Carmel prescribes that Carmelties "pray always," which then presumes they will always listen, first.

In the eleven years between her Baptism and her entrance into Carmel, Edith Stein had already practiced this "apostolate" of listening and praying. The difference lay in that, as a teacher, she was personally available and approachable. Her students and friends, even the slightest acquaintances, could testify to her readiness at all times to give her full attention to anyone who came to her.

Now, in Carmel, she was going one step further in expressing her personal confidence in God. She no longer had to hear the stories of need; in her silent day in Carmel she could include all those who would have sought her out in their need, and she could include the myriads of others whose needs were even greater and more urgent and who did not know where to find support.

Edith had such a living trust in God for all of her nine years in Carmel. Yet she showed this belief externally and unmistakably as soon as she appeared at the enclosure door in Cologne-Lindenthal's monastery. It was the moment of greatest change in her external lifestyle, and for that reason it was captured for her memory by a brief ceremony.

There is a specific symbolic content to this ceremony. The progression of steps carried out so simply outlines in capsule form the whole future life of the woman who chooses to live according to the Rule of the Nuns of the Order of Our Lady of Mount Carmel. It is a form of birth into the religious family less canonical than profession, which is the definitive moment of incorporation.

Until that moment of commitment arrived, Edith, as postulant and novice, could recall what took place the day she entered. Her reception at the enclosure door symbolized her entrance into a contemplative lifestyle.

She stood, momentarily, before the closed door which marked the boundaries of the cloister, awaiting its opening by the superior of the nuns. The Prioress brought along her Council, three nuns elected by the community to be her advisors in situations which affected the whole community. These four nuns could not be considered "in loco parentis" in this case, for the relationship, or contract, one might say, was a personal one between God and Edith, the aspiring religious.

The Order does not *own* its members; it is made up of them and they have an inherent equality clearly expressed in the Rule: "one *of you* shall be prior(ess)," and that one is chosen by an election in which each professed religious has an equal vote.

Once the Prioress and Council had admitted Edith into the enclosure, she knelt down, expressing her relationship to God, and the action of the Prioress in extending the crucifix symbolized the function of a human representative in our relationship with God. He does not deal in mysterious fashion through signs or visions; He uses persons to mediate his involvement in our lives: "who hears you, hears me."

Edith, by kissing the crucifix at that moment clearly expressed her intention, her orientation. She had come to live this life as a personal love-relationship with God. For, when the Son of God, as she believed, became incarnate, he proved his love for her by his death on the cross. Now, her kiss was a pledge of reciprocated love and predilection. She chose him and gave him her exclusive love. This was expressed, symbolically, as the nuns took the postulant, for the first time, to the Choir where the Blessed Sacrament was reserved.

Here, the word "choir" must be understood in a new sense. Rather than the loft or section of a church where the liturgy is sung, the Nuns' Choir in Carmel is the room, usually adjoining the public Chapel, in which they gather for the recitation of the Divine Office.

In 1933, the enclosure regulations provided that the nuns be separated from the altar in the sanctuary of the Church by a wall in which grated openings allowed them to attend liturgical services without being seen by anyone present in the Chapel, including the celebrant. Since Vatican II and its renewal of liturgy, there have been appropriate adaptations in the external expression of enclosure for contemplative nuns. Since this is so, it is well in one study of Edith Stein's years in Carmel to make specific mention of what may otherwise be overlooked.

Edith had a remarkable devotion to the Eucharist, as is clearly seen from her own letters. Friends, students, and Sisters who belonged to the religious communities in Speyer and Münster, all remarked on her frequent, lengthy periods of silent prayer before the Blessed Sacrament.

For eleven years, Edith had attended Mass daily when at all possible; she had, in Speyer, a favorite corner in which her prie-dieu or kneeling bench was set. Here she had a full view of the altar and the celebrant. Now, in Carmel, she was to find herself at Mass, kneeling behind a grille and wearing over her face a veil which obscured even the little that might be visible from one's place so far from the altar. This represented a true deprivation for her.

In the first hour of arrival, at the start of her Carmelite existence, then, she was introduced to this room, the nuns' choir, there to have a moment of prayer. It was another opportunity to make a deliberate choice of this lifestyle and to express in private, personal conversation with the Lord, present in the Sacrament, that all would be gratefully accepted from His hand, echoing the Son's words: "Yes, Father, for so it seems good to you."

The brief moment spent at the side altar where a statue of Our Lady identified the religious community as daughters of the Queen Beauty of Carmel symbolized the postulant's offering herself under the protection and patronage of her model in the religious life, Mary of Nazareth and of Calvary.

Once the many aspects of the life to which Edith had pledged herself were duly expressed, the nuns and Edith went to the recreation room where the postulant was received by the entire community. The warm hug from each one in turn may have surprised Edith, but it was a welcome surprise.

Edith, in her professional years, was generally reserved especially with persons whom she was meeting for a first time; one expects she had to make an almost lightning adjustment on this occasion. However, it is clear from her own account of the years she spent in the Cologne novitiate that all these customs and observances were full of symbolism for her, even if remembering them in detail presented her with the only problems she had.

Her experience in the postulancy and in the first year of her novitiate was typical, in most ways like that of every newcomer. She sensed the unspoken warmth with which the community received her, and the mutual process of becoming acquainted was welcome to this warm-hearted, serious woman. She found herself more spontaneous, more nearly exuberant, than at any other time in her life. She herself said that she laughed more in her first year in Carmel than in the whole of her life before that time.

Frequently, one hears the comment that Edith Stein must have been rather a morose individual. As indication of such a presumed ever-serious disposition her photographs are mentioned. She always appeared unsmiling, almost discontented. The discontent was real, but it had to do only with being photographed. Her disinclination to pose for the camera was legendary, and the almost sulky thrust of her chin, with its deep cleft, is so common to her photos that the rare exceptions are all the more charming. If only an informal snapshot had been taken during the lively recreations when laughter was so spontaneous and so hearty as to draw tears!

Once the community had met Edith, she was conducted to her own private room, called in those days "the cell," not as in a prison, but as in the Latin *cella*, or "a one-room dwelling occupied by a solitary person." This privacy was guaranteed by the Rule so that each nun was undisturbed by the presence of another, and dormitories were never found in Carmels.

14

A Place Apart

Each one shall stay in or near his cell meditating day or night on the law of the Lord unless otherwise justly employed.

-From the Rule

Edith Stein was familiar with the simplicity of the room which was assigned to her within the monastery. It was small, with plain white walls; its window looked out over the cloister garden. The furnishings were sparse: a simple table, a backless seat, and, in the corner, a low wooden bed. The mattress was stuffed with straw; the sheets and blankets were all of rough wool; an earthenware basin and pitcher for washing were at hand, also. An unpretentious wooden cross, a clay holy-water font, and unframed paper prints of Sts. Teresa and John of the Cross, founders of Carmel, adorned the walls.

Altogether, it reminded her of her living quarters with the Dominican Sisters in Speyer, and later, at the Marianum in Münster. But it had one enormous advantage over those other rooms. They had been guest quarters; this room was given her because she belonged to the community.

In general, the daily routine was also similar to the one she had followed in her former positions. Unfamiliar responsibilities and additional activities on the schedule made her first weeks both a joy and a source of bafflement. To her friend,

Hedwig Conrad-Martius, Edith admitted that the most difficult aspect of her postulancy had been the necessity to learn
the customs, the bits of ceremonial that awaited her at every
turn.

When she had arranged her own schedule during her
teaching days, it had been a simple matter to pray the Divine
Office from the Latin breviary, for instance. Now, she had to
get into the routine of turning to face the altar for the beginning
prayer of the Hours, then revert to her former position facing
the opposite choir, all before inclining for the doxology. If she
had a versicler's or the chantress' duties at the Office, she had
to remember when to go to the center of the Choir for an
intonation. She had to know whether to make a full or a
semi-inclination, how much of and when to intone an antiphon
or a psalm.

For someone long accustomed to praying calmly through
the Divine Office with nothing to take her mind off the recitation of the psalms, or of the meaning of the feast which was
being commemorated, the multiple new details could become
an irritating distraction. But Edith's gratitude for being in
Carmel at last was sincere, and putting up with small incon-
veniences was worth it all in her estimation.

A different matter was that of helping with the everyday
chores involved in the orderly maintenance of the monastery.
The work was shared by all in the community; sweeping,
cleaning, and sewing made up a large part of the work assignments while one was in the novitiate. Usually, a newcomer in
the community was named assistant to one of the professed
nuns who would serve as tutor for the sewing or other work if
the postulant was not sufficiently adept at the task.

At her home in Breslau, we have seen, the household was
managed with great ease by one or other of Edith's elder
sisters. Rose Guttmann shared rooms with Edith in Göttingen,
and Rose was clearly put out at the notion that Edith was a
total stranger to housework. In Göttingen, Rose wrote later,
Edith was as good a housekeeper as one could wish. However,
the social order of the time had created almost a cult of cleanli-
ness in homes and in monasteries of nuns, as well. Doing
housework to one's own satisfaction is a far cry from matching
the skill of another woman who has had years of practice, and

who may well have completely forgotten her own initial ineptness.

Edith admitted that when she and Erna were children they thoroughly disliked being ordered to dust or to dry the dishes. It may be far more accurate to identify the object of their dislike: being *ordered* to perform such services. Having them assigned to one in Carmel did not amount to the same thing as being ordered to do them. However, her desire at least to be useful increased her chagrin at her ineptitude. Her individuality in doing the work was as evident to Edith herself as to her companions.

Her autobiographical writings give the impression that everyone in her family assumed she had been spoiled as a child and was therefore, all thumbs when household duties were concerned. Now that her initiation as a religious was of the utmost importance, the inexperience with housework becomes an asset in a surprising respect. It becomes a veritable ill wind that blows her a heap of good things!

The concentration in novitiate training on getting to know and accept oneself with total candor about one's pluses and minuses is a mystery to those unfamiliar with the freedom that comes from such knowledge. Acquiring that freedom is a fulltime program for "spiritual fitness". If one had no weak points, it would almost become necessary to manufacture them in order to learn to accept reality and live one's personal truth. To actually have an area which gave one the opportunity to exercise one's "spiritual muscles" was an advantage. In Carmel, she learned to accept and forget her limitations, tried to keep them from complicating life in community.

In this practical sense, then, embarrassing though it was, the awkwardness with housework was not all bad news for Edith when it surfaced during her first weeks in the monastery. The Sisters, especially her companions in the novitiate, all of whom were some twenty years younger than Edith, found themselves more amused by her lack of skill than displeased. Her own attitude prevented any unpleasantness. But a quarter of a century later, the nuns could recall readily her unique way of mopping the corridors, in one sister's words: "It was almost like taking a pet dog for a walk. She would pull the mop along beside her, clutching it with one hand, confident that the dirt on the floor would stick to it and come along."

What her mother was unable to give by way of maternal training was, after many years, used in God's "maternal" providence to provide his daughter with an unsought mortification. We find Edith's own sentiment expressed to a friend in a letter written about this aspect in her Carmelite life:

> Each day, I take whatever comes, and pray only that the necessary abilities be given me for whatever is required of me. In any case, it is a prime school of humility when you constantly find the things it is your duty to do are accomplished in a very imperfect manner, despite your having completed them with such great effort.

Again, to learn the effect her day-to-day experience in Carmel had on Edith Stein's spirituality, one must recall that the very details of life in the monastery were regulated almost to the limit which could possible be applied. It was not a case of a superior's need to manage or rule, expressing itself by regulating everything "as an obligation" down to minutest detail. The original idea was as brilliant as any efficiency expert might produce, except that efficiency was not the motivation for the minute scheduling. The lifestyle of Carmel witnessed from the beginning to the creative genius of Teresa of Jesus who founded the monastery of St. Joseph, in Avila, Spain, in the sixteenth century.

There was a reason for the thoroughness with which even the minor activities of the Carmelites' days were planned and scheduled. The sole purpose was to free the nuns from having to make anew, at every turn during the day, decisions regarding daily essential tasks. By setting up a schedule for doing these things simply but well, eliminating fuss and annoyance, Teresa intended to foster the life of prayer. Learning to do each task in its way at its time was to become second nature, and so the nuns' psychic and physical energy would be left free to become immersed in an ever deeper spiritual life.

Because the normalcy of such action escapes us, all the "rules" seem an infringement of one's dignity. The contrary is true. Once peripheral skills are learned, one can forget about them and simply go on. So, in Teresa's monasteries, the nuns were intended to learn how to do the daily chores so much as a matter of course that these got done effortlessly. But human nature being what it is, somewhere along the line, new chores were added without dropping outmoded old ones, and life became cluttered with too many time-consuming tasks done because that was custom. In monasteries, often, labor-saving devices were not acquired because of expense, and, frequently then, persons entering religious life found themselves using inefficient methods simply because the nuns had not the means, or the desire, to keep up to date. Then the minute scheduling turned into a burden and it no longer had the freeing effect Teresa wished to provide for her daughters. But years passed before the dynamic was noticed, and even more before its negative effect was understood. Edith's generation in Carmel was precisely the one that brought about the awareness, and in the Cologne community, she is remembered for her part in it.

When Carmel's regulations were written in sixteenth century Spain, most household tasks were tedious and often, time consuming. Spinning and weaving were necessary occupations for women everywhere since clothing was made at home. When religious communities were founded, the same kind of work was included in the daily schedule since the group had to provide for all the members' needs.

A glance at the writings of St. Teresa is all that is needed to see how these indispensable duties were incorporated into the daily life of the nuns. When they received visitors, for instance, it was ordinary for them to take their spindles along to the *speakroom* in order to produce the quota of yarn they knew was required for the making of the nuns' clothes. That their industry even while visiting with family and friends gave witness to their poverty was a fringe benefit. Without electricity, work after sundown was doubly difficult since they hardly had an opportunity to get well-made glasses to compensate for poor sight. This was another incentive to work diligently while there was sufficient light.

When inventions and the growth of industries throughout Europe changed the standard of living in every phase of life, the nuns were less affected by it than their families. The lifestyle in Carmel remained simple and many chores continued to be performed in the customary fashion, not in revolt against progress but because there was no real necessity to change. But, gradually, electricity and appliances found their way into the enclosure, and new methods of cooking, sewing, and washing cut working times amazingly.

In the monastery in Cologne by the time Edith Stein was received, there was a limited amount of "manual labor" to keep all the nuns occupied. Yet, they wished to comply with the Rule, and with St. Teresa's Constitutions.

The legislation was clear; during the hours not given to prayer or meditation, everyone was to be engaged in some form of manual labor. If anyone were unwilling to work, the Rule said they were not to eat! Occupation was good for the heart and mind, as well as for the efficient running of a household.

The nuns in Cologne, in 1933, did not weave baskets like the desert fathers of old, only to take them apart at the end of the day. Nor, like their Spanish sisters of the sixteenth century, did they make woolen or flaxen materials. Industrially produced fabrics had long ago come into ordinary use in Germany. World War I affected monasteries of nuns just as it did their families.

Many homes were bereft of fathers and sons. Factories and shops gave employment to widows and orphans, but the kind of work they did could not be brought into monasteries. Again, St. Teresa had discouraged her daughters from having common workrooms, since the presence of several nuns engaged in a joint enterprise would surely lead to talk and the silence so vital for recollection would be hard to maintain. So the nuns continued their habitual way of living, and worked at making their own clothing, including their braided hempen sandals. They also kept up gardening, if they had ground enough, growing vegetables for the table, canning and preserving what they could. If their location permitted, chickens were raised for eggs, and a cow might provide milk for butter, country cheese and cream, all so important to the nuns' meatless diet. The Carmel in Cologne-Lindenthal had only the vegetable garden.

How did Edith adjust to these circumstances? We recall her reminiscing about her mother's tiny garden in Breslau. We never heard of Edith doing any gardening herself. But she certainly was accustomed to frugality. It was so habitual to her that even after her mother's enterprising labor gained the family a relatively well-to-do lifestyle, Edith tells us she did not change her preferences. She was accustomed to simple foods, at times, indeed, fasting. Her clothes were almost plain, for her principal concern was to live simply though not miserly, and, when she remembered to do so, to dress in keeping with her state in life.

Edith's willingness and preference for doing without certain things herself in order to help less fortunate persons made her welcome a similar attitude expressed in the legislation of Carmel. The nuns were urged to work in order to be able to help the needy, an unselfish reason to keep occupied at all times. Therefore, all her energy was put at the service of the community. However, there was one aspect of work which Edith had never experienced: keeping busy for the sake of the busyness. Should she ever have to look for some kind of occupation, her choice would always be for work that made sense.

With all this in mind, one understands the mixed emotions with which she discovered that the community had gotten into a peculiar bind about their work. Whatever activity was available seemed to be exploited to consume the very last shred of energy the sisters had.

Strangely, since there was never talk about it, the nuns almost seemed house-proud. They would have been shocked at the accusation of vanity in keeping everything as spotless as possible. For Edith, an element of frustration cropped into the work she was given to do. Some of the household tasks assigned were obviously necessary, and for these she expended her best efforts even while she admitted at the end that the will had been great, but the results unfortunate.

However, should she be given a task that had no real purpose other than to occupy time, it was a true penance for her to keep at it. Fortunately, a return to professional writing was judged to be best for Edith, the happiest choice possible.

Naturally, Edith's religious superiors recognized her abilities. Soon after her admission to the novitiate, she was asked to resume her writing. Other tasks were given her as well. These Edith accepted with equanimity, even the instances of "working for the sake of work" that cropped up.

It had become a habit in the Cologne Carmel to scrub all the furnishings of the monastery, once and sometimes twice a year. It began during a year when an occupation had to be invented, so to say. Soon, through repetition, it became an annual project during which each piece of furniture was emptied of whatever contents it had; then, laboriously, it was lugged to the ground floor, by woman-power, to the roomy wash-kitchen. Here, it was scrubbed with as much good will and traditional elbow-grease as though it bore the grime of a century. No doubt, the first time, the improvement was remarkable. But in subsequent years, it was largely time spent needlessly.

Such make-work measures were a source of concern to Edith's generation of nuns. A similar clinging to habitual ways in housework was responsible in some American monasteries for extraordinary work customs which needed to be ended, for they had no relation at all to the quality of the spiritual life of the nuns. This was, fortunately, a passing phase for the Carmels. The aspect most to be deplored about such a development was that only the first generation of nuns engaged in such cleaning sprees knew the purpose was "to have some work to do." When gradually, useful tasks were found, the old "created" ones were a habit, and new sisters coming into the community mistakenly took them to be customs to be preserved as the "Carmelite way of doing things."

With others in her community, Edith joined in the task during her formation years. However, truthful as ever, she was also one of those fully determined to promote and support changes once she was among the community's decision makers, after her profession.

Some of the nuns, in community for years, were unaware that many of the customs followed so faithfully were, in part, an accretion of accidental, temporary measures taken for reasons valid and necessary at one time. However, they had been repeated instead of being discontinued as soon as the reason for them had gone. These nuns found it difficult to accept changes which seemed motivated by a dislike for housework, and there were frank exchanges of opinion.

Had Edith been able to complete her autobiographical work,

we should certainly have come upon some refreshing accounts of her life and involvement in matters in which the community's Chapter made decisions about the kind of manual labor to undertake. She would have recorded the criticisms expressed to her by those who felt threatened by "innovations" or rash changes in time-hallowed practices. Again, this was the same dynamic which was occurring in homes and schools, and places of employment all over the world. In some sense, it was progress.

To consider that Edith could have become suddenly spineless out of a mistaken understanding of the role of a religious is to do her a disservice. Likewise, to think she was treated like a mindless individual who had to be told each moment what must be done would be just as false. St. Teresa was justifiably confident that her daughters would continue to use common sense in making necessary adjustments of their Carmelite life. She trusted them to assess their activities often, over the years, in such a way that the priorities she herself set up would rule their lives.

Edith understood that to be a true daughter of Teresa, she needed to be faithful, in Carmel, to her own sound common sense, and to offer the best of her intelligent assessment of each situation with respect but without hesitation, even in the face of the disapproval of some of her companions. Those who lived with her in those five years at Cologne are unanimous in giving that kind of a picture of her, stressing always that she had a remarkable gentleness of character which enabled her to be very firm in a dissenting opinion while remaining as friendly and courteous as one could wish.

For her and her sisters, the unpleasantness and unrest which was to upset their lives came from the political storms outside, and these made the normal human frictions inside become stepping stones for loving interaction among sisters.

15

Pray Always, Meditating Day or Night

Teresa of Jesus was a religious for years before she became convinced that in the Monastery of the Incarnation in Avila, Spain, she could not find the silence and solitude that would allow her to give her full attention to God in prayer. In her writings she says she was comfortable in the large though crowded community. But there were too many comings and goings for one who was increasingly aware of a call from God to live more deeply in union with Him.

Therefore, with several companions she finally decided that so busy a house created many distractions for the nuns. On August 24, 1562, these foundresses established a small house, St. Joseph's Monastery, also in Avila.

To the Rule which the entire Carmelite Order observed, constitutions were now added as legislation. The distinctive and innovative feature was the right given each individual nun to have two hours of her day free for prayer. This hallmark of Teresa's was faithfully preserved in her foundations.

In a case of necessity, some occupation which could not be postponed or neglected might call for an exception, which was then handled intelligently. However, it was also the rule that no work assignment could be given which would frequently interfere with the two hours for prayer called for in the daily schedule. In the three centuries between Teresa's time and the day Edith entered the Cologne community on October 14, 1933, there was no significant change in the daily regimen.

Edith joined other women who were in various stages of formation. Her instruction in Carmelite living was given to her individually, not as a member of the group. This was the usual manner of introducing postulants to their responsibilities; of course, the whole group at times received conferences in class. When the young Sisters of the Cologne community were introduced to the new postulant, they were already a mixed group. Those in formation included both lay and choir sisters. The distinction between them was that "choir" nuns assumed the obligation to recite daily the liturgical hours of the Divine Office, the Church's official prayer.

Like many other Catholics who privately included extra prayer in their lives, Edith had been praying the breviary for years. The "Hours" were planned in such a way that during any given week, one prayed all of the 150 Psalms found in the Old Testament. Since Vatican Council II, some adaptation has excluded a few of those psalms which called for God's maledictions on one's enemies.

Latin was one of Edith's favorite languages, and as she had taught it in the girls' school in Breslau, she was now allowed to use her knowledge to help the young novices and postulants who were in formation with her. For some it was totally unintelligible, and there was mutual relief when the directress arranged for Edith to help those who had never had any instructions. Five Sisters were in formation in October, 1933, and in her letters during the ensuing months, Edith faithfully mentions whenever one of the quintette has been accepted to receive the habit or to make a profession of vows.

Even though they were in various stages of formation, Edith's companions shared one advantage: all were nearly twenty years younger than Edith. Their educational background was also varied; most had no more than an average of eight to ten years of formal schooling. But some sisters were as well educated as Edith, although not in philosophy, but as teachers.

Her professional background made Edith differ significantly from her companions. We gain an immediate insight into her personality when we hear from her companions that they were largely unaware of her more extensive education. Even her forty-two years of age had not been specifically noticed by the much younger novices and postulants with whom Edith spent so many hours in her first four years in Carmel.

Entrance into the contemplative life of Carmel does not magically endow a woman with infallible qualities of mind and heart nor will it add any new fallible ones. She brings herself with any plus or minus, as she is, to Carmel and the time in formation is provided for her and for the community to see how well someone with precisely her positive or negative qualities can be integrated in the group. If the prognosis is favorable, the pace of the integration is also tailored to each individual. Coercion is out of the question; the life is freely chosen. Should a candidate be unhappy, she may freely leave at any time.

The principal personal qualification which Teresa told her nuns to seek in a postulant is *common sense* and the Nuns have made this almost a rule of thumb in Carmel. Every monastery's history, of course, is a record of human interaction. So, in Carmel, there are turbulent times; yet, when the sea is stormy, there is no need to panic. These are the deep yet marvelous waters of prayer, communal and individual. To channel her life in these waters was what Edith sought and found in Carmel.

From the beginning of her formation, Edith discovered one distinct difference in her lifestyle. Exteriorly it seemed very much like her daily routine at either Speyer or Münster, if one excepted her teaching activity. However, formerly it was entirely by her own choice that she mingled with the other teachers, or with the students at St. Magdalene's and the Marianum. When she preferred to be alone, she simply remained in her own quarters. Now, in Carmel, she experienced what it means to live like a "hermit but in community."

The development of the monastic life as it is presented by the Rule of Carmel may be described as a combination of the eremitic with the cenobitic life. It may be said that the best of both lifestyles has been preserved: the silence and solitude of the desert fathers has been joined to the common life of the early monks. But if the advantages of both are available, so are the hazards. The combination demands maturity in an individual; moderate balance is required so that neither seclusion nor the common life is stressed at the expense of the other.

From Cologne, Edith wrote to one of her friends, who had worried about her adjustment, "In my life here, I miss nothing that I had formerly; and I find here everything that I missed formerly."

Precisely what did she find? How does one understand the Rule when it is applied to flesh and blood—and specifically as when it affects the person of Edith, not some imaginary, possible candidate for the life? The uncomplicated areas into which the day's activities can be separated enable us to estimate much of what Edith's life provided, and what it demanded of her.

Numerically, the day was divided evenly: seven hours of prayer, seven of work, seven of sleep; the remaining three provided time to eat and to have recreation. The prayer, again, was of three forms. First, there was liturgical prayer: the Eucharist and the Hours, or Mass and the Divine Office in pre-Vatican II terminology. Second, there was the mental prayer in community, the two hours already mentioned. Finally, at various times of the day, vocal prayers, such as the Litany of Loreto, prayers at meals, and brief commemorations of the Saints of the Order, were also recited in common. In their free hours, each one added to these her personal prayers of private devotion, be they vocal, such as the rosary, or contemplative, such as mental prayer, recollection, and reflection. This was the warp and woof of Edith's day; all other activities were supported by prayer, or preparation for it.

The customs provided that every Sister, if she were willing, discussed her prayer with the superior, not in the sense of having to *produce* something, nor for the sake of a critical appraisal of whatever she may have experienced in her prayer, but as an aid to greater progress. It is possible to miss significant signposts in our own situations; we can benefit from the advice of another who lives with us and recognizes how we are responding to God and his gifts.

Edith Stein was no "beginner" in prayer by the time she entered Carmel. Many who knew her during her years in Speyer were aware of the long hours which she was in the habit of spending, kneeling motionless before the Eucharist in the school or convent chapel. Here we find one sacrifice which Carmel asked of Edith. She was no longer able to remain at prayer for so many hours at a time. Now she had the regular schedule to follow. She does not mention this loss but it must have been a keen one.

How shall one comment on Edith's prayer since she says little enough about it? Perhaps all that needs to be said is to repeat her own brief phrase, "My secret is mine." When she read the life of Teresa of Avila, Edith learned Teresa's definition of prayer: a conversation between two who love one another. In Carmel, one's primary responsibility and occupation is to establish a deep personal relationship with God and to nurture it by constant, interior, and usually silent, conversation with Him. There is no self-seeking nor self-serving involved. Edith was aware that the topics she brought into her talks with God were not to be exclusively petitions for some assistance or other.

The catechism she had studied so assiduously before her Baptism told her that there are four objectives in praying: to offer God praise; to give him thanks for His love and His gifts; to make reparation for our wilful or even our inadvertent shortcomings; and, finally, to present our petitions for further assistance.

Just as an horizon can never hem us in, so there are no boundaries in a life dedicated to a prayer-relationship with God. For the philosopher who learned from everyone and every situation in which she found herself, the realization that infinity lay open to her in her relationship with God was a heady discovery. Then the question arises, since Edith wrote so lucidly on questions of philosophy, why not more on prayer? She had a feeling that she was called on to teach philosophy; a similar call to "teach" prayer is never mentioned. What she felt called upon to make known at every opportunity was "how to live at God's hand", and this is a perfect form of prayer expressed in action, not in words. Her prayer, then, can be deduced from her behavior, her demeanor. No wonder she is likened to the familiar depiction in the art of the early Christian Church, the woman with arms raised in prayer, the "Ecclesia Orans." For many who had observed her at prayer in Speyer, in the Abbey of Beuron, or in Carmel, Edith was prayer personified.

A further reason for her reticence may have to do simply

with "words." We know that discoveries in the natural order cannot always be shared fully because there is not yet a proper language in which to express one's knowledge. Often, then, in a prayer relationship it is simply beyond one's human capacity to put the experience in words.

Can we ever speak of her "way"? She who in her lifetime walked on so many lovely paths in the mountains, often without a guide, was content to go her way to God without leaving a trail for others to follow readily. But we have dependable signs to show it to us, nevertheless. The example of one who lives an authentic prayer life is enough, for "by their fruits you will know them".

Carmelite spirituality has been from the first days of Teresa of Jesus and John of the Cross inseparable from an intense, personal love for Jesus Christ. In the *Book of my Life*, which led Edith Stein to see a Carmelite vocation as an integral part of her reception in the Catholic Church, St. Teresa gives incident after incident of the depth of her personal experience of Christ's love. Another Carmelite nun, the French Thérèse of Lisieux, was becoming known in Edith's time. Her "little way" of spiritual childhood was once more a simple relationship of the person with God, her Father.

Edith Stein spent nearly as many years in Carmel's cloister as had Thérèse of the Child Jesus. Both of them had experienced opposition from the competent authorities to their entering Carmel. Thérèse wished to enter at fifteen years of age; Edith said her vocation was given her at the time of her reception of Baptism. Devotion to the Eucharistic Presence was the center of both their lives.

Therese Martin spent fifteen years as the darling of her widowed father. The nine years she lived in Carmel found her teaching spiritual childhood as the way to go to God, her Father. Her "public life" began after her death and her "little way" was offered to all.

Edith Stein, for eleven years after her Baptism, led a very busy "public life" giving lectures all over German-speaking Europe. She became an influential, highly visible, articulate, and determined witness to her faith. She, who as a two-year old had lost her father, did not concentrate on *calling* God "father," but her attitude toward him was in every sense that of a totally dependent, trusting child, with open hands and grateful heart.

She had no doubt about having a message for the Church and for the whole world. Whether she was commended or criticized for it, she had an unalterable aim during her teaching and lecturing years: to communicate as clearly as she could that one thing alone is necessary. We must receive all we have and all that happens to us as coming from the hands of God.

In her years at Speyer and Münster, she impressed her hearers with the importance, the necessity, of teaching children that basic lesson: all comes from God. Family, friends, country, and the personal riches of health, happiness, rewarding work, recreation and fun, all come from the beneficent hand of God. They must be accepted with gratitude and accountability. She constantly reminded teachers and parents of their responsibility to prepare the young for life by helping them to have receptive, grateful hearts. Now, in Carmel, she lived that doctrine, and prayed for all whom she had ever met, asking for them the same grace of knowledge she had received.

16

Consider the Lilies

It is not unusual for one who enters Carmel to experience a newness of life. This was true for Edith Stein, and it was apparent to those who observed her during her first year in Cologne. She knew an almost therapeutic release of the joyousness that was inherently hers but which had been rather subdued even in her childhood. Now she could be herself, her full, richly endowed self among her youthful companions.

In the Carmelite life they were all beginners, but the variety of experience they brought to this communal living made for fascinating interaction. For most of the day, they worked, prayed, or studied together in a silence that avoided all unnecessary speaking. The daily schedule arranged according to the Constitutions seldom varied:

> In summer, they are to rise in time to be in choir at five, and they are to remain there in prayer until six; in winter, they are to go to choir at six, and remain in prayer until seven.
>
> Prayer being ended they are to recite the Canonical Hours—either all together, or one or two may be postponed until before the Conventual Mass, as the Prioress shall decide, but all the hours are to be said before Mass begins....
>
> The hours being over, each one shall go to her respective duties or office....
>
> At two o'clock in the afternoon, Vespers are to be said, after which they are to read some spiritual book; but Vespers

and reading are not to take up more than an hour. If,
through fervor of spirit, they desire to spend the time for
reading in prayer, they may do what shall seem best for
their spiritual recollection.

The hour of prayer, which takes place at five o'clock in
the evening, should precede supper or collation, that being
the most suitable time for this duty.

As may be seen from this horarium, about seven hours of
Edith's day were spent in her own room. In the first months
the postulants usually filled this time by engaging in some
ordinary and monotonous tasks. During the years Edith taught
at Speyer, some friends of hers protested, appalled at the
thought of the number of hours she spent in correcting
students' written assignments. These same persons would have
been scandalized at seeing her now, laboriously stitching away
at some sewing. Although one of her aunts had initiated her at
the age of five in that homely art, Edith never had enough
practice at it to become a proficient seamstress.

The Sisters who lived with Edith unanimously remarked on
her absolute willingness to accept any task, and to learn those
simple household techniques with which she had so little experience of late. If her sewing was not expert, at least, they said
she was speedy at it.

The Mistress of Novices, who is known in post-Vatican
days by the more accurate title of Directress of Formation,
usually assigned duties to the Sisters and if they needed instruction in carrying them out, she supplied that, too. Once, she
showed Edith how to assemble small "relic cases"—devotional
articles prepared to serve as souvenirs for visitors to the monastery, or as enclosures in the community letters to persons who
wrote asking the nuns' prayers for special intentions.

Edith diligently sewed and accumulated her handiwork until
she could present fifty of the small mementos to the Novice
Mistress. They proved to be lovingly but poorly sewn. The
buttonhole embroidery stitches were unaligned, and so the
Mistress quietly gave them to one of the senior Sisters in the
novitiate to fix. That novice, an accomplished seamstress
hardly more than twenty years old, was far from thrilled at the
quiet repair job she had to do. It would have taken her less

time and effort to make new souvenirs than to unpick and resew Edith's.

The Sisters in Cologne who were in the novitiate with Edith in those first years recounted the incident with warm sympathy and affection for both the postulant and the novice. On February 15, 1934, as was the custom when a newcomer had completed four months as a postulant, the nuns gathered in Chapter to vote whether she should be admitted to further formation as a novice. To make certain that the postulant freely desired to become a novice, the vote on such occasions was taken only after the postulant made a formal request in the presence of the entire community. Accordingly, after being brought into the assembly by the Mistress of Novices, Edith knelt in the center of the Chapter Room to ask for acceptance, using the formula provided in the custom books of the Monastery. With slight local variations in the terminology, the petition was alike in all Carmels:

> I humbly beg your Reverence and the Community to have the charity, for the love of God, to admit me to the Holy Habit, although I am most unworthy of it. I shall do all in my power to be a cause of consolation to the community.

Since the Second Vatican Council, many of the customs which had existed in religious communities for centuries have been modified or discontinued. To evaluate Edith Stein's experiences in Carmel between 1933 and 1942, it seems particularly useful to preserve a record of some customs or ceremonies in use at the time she entered, for the sake of readers who have no way of knowing what they might have been, as well as for religious, even in Carmelite monasteries, who are no longer familiar with those customs. Such ceremonial gestures were given meaning largely through the devotion of those who participated in them. For Edith, most were new and many may have seemed formalistic, and for someone at her age, they may also have required an acceptance that cost her something.

It must be remembered that she did not complain about them. However, she admitted to Hedwig Conrad-Martius the difficulty she had getting accustomed to some of the daily observances, such as inclinations during the Divine Office, the manner of greeting one another, and some ceremonial actions observed in the refectory. The older nuns, who had become so accustomed to this manner of doing things forgot that they had to be learned, and were unaware of the difficulty they posed for new Sisters. Performed almost by rote, the customs could come to lose their effect. The formal request for admission to the novitiate made a lasting impression because it signified a real beginning, an incorporation into the Order.

This request has no vestige of subservience about it. That it was made while kneeling was a reminder to all that the vocation comes from God and that this petition was made to him, even if it was addressed to the community through whom it would be granted or not. Everyone in the Chapter had at one time made an identical request, and the wording carried no implication that if the one requesting admission considered herself unworthy to wear the habit, those granting it thought themselves worthy. Here, "worthiness" is a concept to be understood in a healthy way as esprit de corps. The votation which followed the formal request was affirmative and the ceremony ended in a most cordial round of congratulations.

For her part, Edith found herself more and more part of the Carmelite family. The other members of the Novitiate rejoiced especially with her. In the four months, they had noticed a great change in her. She seemed to have shed years in their estimation, and her joyous laughter no longer came as a rare surprise. Her sense of humor and of fun enlivened the novitiate recreations, often at her own expense, as she recounted new misadventures in a postulant's progress.

The weeks between her acceptance that day and the ceremony on April 15 were unusual ones for Edith. She became the center of all the activity in the monastery, a phenomenon repeated whenever a Clothing Ceremony is in the offing.

In her account of the family history, Edith told of trousseaus fashioned by her grandmothers, aunts and cousins, all working together to provide one of the brides of the extended family with all she needed for her marriage. Now, the sisters in the Cologne Carmel performed this familial act of love for Edith. Some set about making her habit, veil, white toque or coif, her brown scapular and the white mantle. Others fashioned the braided, hempen alpargates, as the sandals were called, the familiar symbol of the *Discalced* Carmelite nuns. New linens were also made, along with the rough woolen tunic or under-garment, the brown woolen handkerchiefs used at Cologne, and the heavy-beaded rosary worn suspended from the leathern cincture. All this called for repeated fittings, now in one "officine", then in another. For Edith, most comfortable when she was unnoticed among her companions, this attention was novel but she knew how to receive as well as to give.

Since she was spontaneously generous in offering whatever assistance she could give to her sisters, she now gracefully accepted their ministrations. In this simple exchange between the sisters, one has another indication that Edith felt herself truly one of this Carmelite family. Formerly, for more than two decades of her life, she had known the complete indepen-dence to which her professional status entitled her. Exchanging it for a new mode of living in community, and doing this easily, demonstrated how much of herself she had invested in Carmel.

A bridal dress was customarily worn for the Clothing Ceremony. Edith's was made of a heavy white silk sent from Breslau as Rosa's gift to Edith. (Providentially, this gown was made into a vestment which, during the air raids, was safely stored with sacristy items so it remained undamaged by the bombing. This same vestment, reworked for the occasion, was worn by Pope John Paul II for the Liturgy on May 1, 1987, when Edith Stein was declared blessed.) Many of Edith's friends who attended the Ceremony at her invitation remarked on her radiant joy during the celebration.

There had been little evidence, during Edith's first six months in Carmel, of the esteem with which she continued to be regarded in the academic world. Now, on this Good Shepherd Sunday, numerous friends, most of them well-known in university circles throughout the German-speaking coun-tries, came to share with Edith the joy and consolation of her reception into the Order.

In the Cologne Carmel, a postulant who was to receive the habit went into the monastery's public chapel for the Mass, to be with her relatives and friends. Edith, surrounded by familiar persons seemed oblivious to everything and everyone except the ceremonies at the altar and the worship offered to God by all who were attending, united with her in grateful and joyous response to the Lord. .

Sunday, April 15, was the big day. Forty years later, Sr. Maria Baptista Pohl still had a vivid recollection of this occasion when Edith was clothed in the habit of a daughter of Teresa of Jesus in the Discalced Carmelite Order.

Precisely at that time, this young lady, born in Cologne, was asking the nuns to receive her. Her parish priest knew Edith Stein whom he had met during one of her lecture tours. He told his parishioner, the prospective Carmelite, to attend the public ceremony at the Carmel that Sunday morning, and also asked his youthful charge to pray for Edith Stein. The notion that she should be asked to pray for someone who had already achieved the privilege of which she herself was still dreaming impressed the young woman, and she could hardly wait to see what kind of person this Edith Stein might be. So Fräulein Pohl, who would, herself, in time become Sr. Baptista, attended the Clothing Ceremony at Carmel on Sunday, April 15, 1934.

A pontifical High Mass, the most solemn form of public worship in those pre-Vatican II days, was celebrated by the Benedictine Archabbot of Beuron, Dom Raphael Walzer.

Pater Theodorus, Provincial of the German Province of the Discalced Carmelite Fathers, was present to preside at the ceremony. Some of Edith's most cherished friends from Göttingen days attended the festivities.Chief among them was Dr. Hedwig Conrad-Martius, Edith's sponsor at Baptism. Dr. Elisabeth Cosack who had presented Edith's request for acceptance at Carmel to the nuns some seven months earlier was there, of course. Former students whom Edith had taught in Freiburg, Speyer or Münster came to testify to the value placed on Edith's friendship by those who had known her in school.

After officiating at the High Mass, Dom Raphael spoke to the congregation. His warm words of appreciation for Edith's contribution to the Church embarrassed her. Having put all of that activity behind her, she gave little thought to former accomplishments. When Dom Raphael finished speaking, the ritual called for a dialogue between the "bride" and the official representative of the Order of Discalced Carmelites.

> Father Provincial: What do you ask?
> Edith: The mercy of God, the poverty of the Order, and the company of the Sisters.
> Father Provincial: Are you determined to persevere in the Order until death?
> Edith: Thus do I hope and desire, through the mercy of God and the prayers of the Sisters.

In the name of the community, Pater Theodorus then prayed, asking God to perfect the work he had begun in this Carmelite Sister, to give her the grace to become the new person her vocation called her to be. As this prayer came to a close, Edith rose from her knees, and, carrying a candle, walked to the door of the cloister which opened to admit her.

Her friends in the public chapel gathered around the grating through which the nuns' choir could be seen. Before Edith entered this room, the wedding dress she had worn at Mass was exchanged for the brown habit of the Carmelite.

The Mistress of Novices led her to the front of the choir where Edith now knelt to receive, one after the other, the cincture, scapular, and white mantle which completed her Carmelite ensemble.

Now the moment had arrived when Edith Stein would receive a new name. Often, this name came as a surprise to a new religious, but in Edith's case, she had been asked her own preference, and it is evident why she chose to be called Teresa Benedicta of the Cross.

The title, a Cruce, was in Latin, and was not used in ordinary conversations, but was always given in her signature, and whenever assignments within the Community were listed. The intention of giving such a title was to express the equality of all the Sisters. Dropping family names in favor of a religious title by adding a patron's name to one's own served admirably in the 16th century to avert partiality or preference because of birth or influence. In Germany, even when Edith entered Carmel, an aristocracy persisted. One Sister in the Cologne Carmel had been the Countess Maria Anna von Praschma. Her name in Carmel was Sister Marianne of God; she was one of the nuns who hoped to found a monastery in Breslau, when that would be possible.

The Cologne nuns had a custom of taking Teresa, in its German form, Teresia, as part of every nun's name. And for Edith, the principal name, *Benedicta*, commemorated the spiritual influence in her life of the Benedictine school of spirituality at the Beuron Archabbey, and of Dom Raphael, her spiritual director.

Edith asked for the title, a Cruce, of the Cross, because this mystery of the Catholic Faith more than any other expressed for her the belief that suffering in this life, of whatever nature it might be, can be united to the suffering of Christ on the Cross. Pain and difficulty are great unifying factors when they are shared with Christ and with all those who, in their own private lives, united themselves in accepting with Christ whatever suffering may come their way.

Despite some clear pointers to her private devotion, there is a challenge to the study of Edith-Benedicta's spirituality. Compared to Teresa of Jesus, Therese of the Child Jesus, or Elizabeth of the Trinity, she was most reticent about her interior life, her intimate relationship with God.

Now Sister Benedicta was no more forthcoming with details than she had been as Edith Stein. One has to glean from remarks in conversations or comments in letters the motivation for her actions and attitudes. This exercise demands a patient study of her legacy in its developing stages.

Edith frequently referred to the years of waiting to enter Carmel, a call she heard clearly at her Baptism. But she made no big issue of it, mentioning it only because of some related circumstance. She was overjoyed when at last her dream was fulfilled. Her comment is poignant, that when a petition she has prayed for, patiently, for a very long time was granted, it seemed to her more "overwhelming" than when she had an immediate answer to prayer.

One part of her dream was not realized: not even Rosa was at the Clothing Ceremony to represent the family. But the bridal dress was a mute witness that her sister was very much aware of the occasion; her other sisters had written to Edith. To spare their Mother a reopening of the wound of separation, Frau Stein was not told of the day's significance. The time had not come yet when she could write notes to her youngest daughter whose love, however, never wavered in its fidelity.

Those among her friends who had been rather estranged at the thought of Edith "behind bars" were pleasantly surprised. They had to admit that after a few minutes they forgot there was a grating between them and their cherished friend whose patent happiness was contagious. The interviews with her friends took place in the *speakroom* which had been built to the specifications handed down in Carmel from the time of Teresa of Jesus:

> The speakroom has a grate in the wall. On the outside, there are crossed iron bars, and spikes are placed at every other crossing of these bars. On the interior side, approximately seventeen inches distant from the iron grate, there is to be a row of wooden dowels. A curtain should hang on the inside, and there should be wooden frames for shutters, with black buckram nailed on them. The shutters should be kept locked.
>
> -From Usages in Conformity with Regulations after Council of Trent

There were long years when Spain's titled families were large, but women in them far outnumbered the men. Sons were off to the New World as soon as they were old enough to be lured by greed for gold or land. Often, the daughters in these families became a burden to relatives too poor to provide a dowry large enough to tempt a young man to find treasure closer to home. The alternative to living with impoverished parents, under circumstances that promised little happiness for an unmarried woman or for her relatives, was to live in a convent with others of similar social rank. These women were taking refuge together, not following a religious vocation. When Teresa of Jesus entered the Convent of the Incarnation at Avila, a good number of the women there had come for just such a reason.

The "Reform" of Carmel meant that Teresa and a few Sisters opened a much smaller convent where only a few nuns would be accepted into the religious family. The interesting aspect to this change was that, often enough, those who begged to be admitted to this stricter form of life were young women whom their relatives wanted to keep, for whom dowries were gladly provided, who were most likely to attract suitors of the better families. To prevent nuns who had been received into the community from being removed by force by their irate relatives, enclosure was strictly enforced. Protection against sword-wielding cavaliers took the form of "crossed iron bars with spikes."

When the historical situation which introduced spiked grilles changed, especially in other countries, the grilles were retained for a presumed symbolism. Persons unaware of the history related to these grates, dowels, curtains, and shutters, did not see them as anachronistic, but as a singular feature of Carmel. Only the nuns themselves, constantly constrained to explain or to excuse them, realized how they actually obscured the true meaning and interpretation of enclosure in our century. Women freely choose religious life, and their right to do so is respected by their families, by civil law, and by the Church; it needs no metal bars to be protected.

In her notes and letters acknowledging the visits, letters, or gifts at her Clothing Ceremony, Sister Benedicta explained to those who had misunderstood the requirements of enclosure that there was no alteration in their relationship.

Fritz Kaufmann, despite being her lifelong friend, had assumed, we know, that Edith's acceptance into the Order, symbolized by her reception of the habit, would signal an end to their correspondence. Within a month of the Clothing Ceremony, he was reassured that Edith was as much his friend as ever. As she had told him in a letter much earlier, nothing would interfere with her relationship to her friends. Once admitted into her life, one was there forever. Herr Kaufmann was going to be able to write to Sister Benedicta, and he was one friend who visited her at the monastery.

Archabbot Walzer, before returning to Beuron after the Clothing Ceremony, had a private visit with Sister Benedicta. Although his laudatory comments about her had been disconcerting, Edith was as honest as always in answering his questions about her experience as a postulant in Carmel.

Dom Raphael was a perceptive spiritual director. His acquaintance with Edith had convinced him, soon after he met her, that he was speaking to someone other than a novice in the ways of spirituality. However, when she expressed her desire to enter a Carmelite monastery soon after her Baptism, he counselled a delay. His experience with the Church's needs in those critical years between the two great wars convinced him that a woman with the talents and the wisdom Edith Stein possessed had a great deal to give to the laity in all the German-speaking lands of Europe. When he finally gave his permission for her entry to the Carmel of Cologne, he wondered how she would adjust to Carmel.

Now, having come to Cologne for the Clothing Ceremony, he would take advantage of the visit to satisfy himself that Edith was at peace in her decision. He would ask her whether she found the adjustment difficult.

He had a conviction that "such a soul that hungered for knowledge and yearned to pursue research" would be uneasy after setting aside all that to live with uncomplicated young women scarcely out of their teens. This assumption was based on his own experience as a Benedictine religious. Had Edith become a Benedictine or a Dominican nun, there would have been scope for her scholarship in channels that seemed alien to Carmel. But, despite her ties to Beuron and Speyer, Edith was determined to become a daughter of Teresa rather than of Benedict or Dominic.

Dom Raphael's question for Sister Benedicta was phrased carefully to show her that a frank admission of difficulties would in no way be misconstrued as a criticism or disparagement of her companions. To it he added a final condition; she was to give her spiritual director an absolute and undiplomatic answer. Her response was immediate and sincere: she was completely at home in heart and spirit. This statement, made in her spontaneous, warm, even lively manner, wiped out any doubt he had. She had truly found the answer to her desires in that community.

It was to be Dom Raphael's last visit to her, by the way, although they kept up a correspondence. The Benedictines of Beuron and their Archabbot had many worries and distractions in the years ahead. Dom Raphael's first impression of Edith's spiritual maturity had been confirmed repeatedly in the five years he was her director. Now that she was in a religious community, her need of a director had lessened. Her daily life was regulated by the Rule and the Constitutions by which all the Carmelites lived. For any extraordinary situations, she would be able to consult either the Mistress of Novices or the Prioress. The Archabbot was confident of having done all that was necessary for his protege; whatever was lacking would come from the Lord. A very happy chapter in Edith's life came to a satisfactory close.

17

In the House of the Lord, All My Days

Novitiate begins with the reception of the Habit.... The year of the novitiate, under the direction of the Mistress, has for its object the forming of the mind of the novices by the study of the Rule and Constitutions, by pious meditations, assiduous prayer, by learning what appertains to the vows and virtues.... The novices must not devote themselves of set purpose to the study of literature, the sciences or the arts....

-Excerpt from the Constitutions

The vitality of the religious life depends, understandably, upon fidelity to the Rule. However, that means being faithful to the spirit rather than to the letter of the Rule, a fidelity demonstrated by a decision Sister Benedicta's prioress, Mother Teresia Renata (Posselt) de Spiritu Sancto, reached soon after her reception of the habit. That Sr. Benedicta resume scholarly study and writing once she was in the novitiate was consistent with the spirit of the Rule even when the letter contained nothing to demand it.

There were several advantages to engaging Sr. Benedicta in her former work. The index to her translation of St.Thomas' *Quaestiones* into German needed to be made, and that was her initial assignment.

This kind of "exceptional" work might have caused among her companions a feeling that Sr. Benedicta was being favored. That it did not do so proved she was given no extraordinary privileges. Nor was she excused from observances to which the rest complied. Her work was considered ordinary although she spent some hours at it while the rest of the community enjoyed the recreation period in common. If it was satisfying to the scholar in her to be back at her philosophical writing, then it was at the same time frustrating to pursue it under the new time schedule.

A maximum of two consecutive hours for work was all she had at one stretch. The bell for some "exercise" such as the recitation of part of the Divine Office, or meals, or community activities, would call a halt just when she was in the midst of some particularly interesting or intricate stage in her work.

If Dom Raphael had any fear that Edith Stein's reputation as a scholar or lecturer had preceded her in this community, the report she gave him on her first year there allayed his misgivings and convinced him that awed reverence was far from what the other members of the novitiate accorded Sister Benedicta. A natural, truly human atmosphere was discernible. There was a healthy amount of grumbling which could be attributed much more to hunger than to vanity. One young sister was overheard, muttering, "Well! the *Doctors* get milk!"

In providing milk for Sr. Benedicta during the season in Carmel when the prescribed fast and abstinence excluded dairy products, the Mistress of Novices had provided Edith with a unique kind of self-denial which did not go unnoticed in the congenial atmosphere of the novitiate. For years, Edith's eating habits were rather hit and miss. She said her mother was glad to have her visit Breslau because for those few days at least, Edith would eat regular meals. When her studies at Göttingen had absorbed her attention, she had grown careless about food. And during the years at Speyer and Münster, the students and the Sisters noticed that Fräulein Stein ate little and seemed to have few preferences at table. Taking milk during the time of the abstinence in Carmel then was more of a hardship than a welcome dispensation for her; but she willingly followed the directions of the Mistress who felt the extra nourishment would do her good.

Sister Benedicta was anything but a sanctimonious, nearly-perfect, stereotypical novice. Her wit was as lively at the age of 42 as it had been in her teens; her gift for mimicry enabled her to copy the behavior and attitudes of her companions in the novitiate so well that those she was teasing felt complimented and joined in the hearty laughter. And when Sr. Benedicta reported on one of her own inexperienced but ever-willing sallies into the complexities of household chores, all of them, including the raconteur, laughed themselves to tears.

One of her memorable blunders which was recounted during a recreation forty years later, with at least as much merriment as it occasioned when it happened, was connected with a procession to honor St. Joseph. The youngest novice could claim the privilege of carrying a statue of the saint to lead a procession of the nuns from the recreation room to the Choir. Sr. Benedicta was as pleased as anyone years younger might have been; she carefully held the statue aloft as the procession headed along the corridors, lowering it only when she passed through the doorway. Inside the Choir, the head of the statue collided with the oil-lamp suspended from the sanctuary ceiling which thereupon tilted, causing the oil to pour over the statue down upon Sr. Benedicta's head, soaking into her veil, and dripping onto her white mantle.

Anyone else would have moved away instinctively, but not this particular "saint-bearer" and erstwhile researcher in psychology! She made a dead stop, looking up into the shower of oil to discover the cause of this unusual anointing. As a result of this mishap, it became an in-house joke to cite, instead of Aaron's beard which the psalmist mentions, Benedicta's veil when speaking of the "oil of brotherhood running down upon . . . . " None laughed more heartily than Sister Benedicta herself at having thus become "the Lord's anointed."

Other indications of her good humor and cheerful acceptance of unflattering situations surfaced whenever the Sisters who lived with her began to reminisce. One of the youngest of their companions used to defend her own viewpoint passionately, no matter what topic was introduced. Sister Benedicta knew exactly how to draw her into a discussion that would entertain the whole group while not belittling or flattering either of the participants. Asked whether they thought of Edith at the time as being "saintly" they were surprised by the question because they had no clear idea how one tells "a saint" from the rest of the crowd; it never occurred to anyone to do so.

One of the nuns who was a lay sister when Edith was in the novitiate thought she had a "formula" according to which Edith did not qualify. "If she was such a holy person, how was it she never came to the kitchen to lend a hand?"

The incongruity of the formula can only be appreciated when one knows that in those years, no one was free to enter anyone else's workroom without special permission from the Mistress of Novices; and all had assignments that precluded voluntary good deeds of this kind. To have acted so contrarily to instructions was anything but behavior to be expected of any novice, least of all Sr. Benedicta.

Her gift for story-telling, so evident to readers of *Life in a Jewish Family*, helped to make recreation a time her young companions anticipated with delight. As an actor in the skits the novices wrote and produced for a Feast Day or some other Community celebration, Sister Benedicta proved her versatility. Whether she was cast as an invisible "voice" of God the Father, or in a costumed part as a beggar, seated in tragicomic contemplation of her empty hat, Sister Benedicta was certain to evoke the proper mood in the audience.

Mother Renata, her Mistress of Novices, appreciated Sr. Benedicta's gifts as a scholar and philosopher; both superior and novice were mature women firmly determined to be generous and faithful to the best of their ability.

In the ordinary situations in community, it was natural for Sr. Benedicta to adjust readily to life with persons so much younger than herself. She had always been gifted with a particularly warm rapport with the young, her own nieces and nephews, first, and then the pupils in the elementary grades whom she taught in Breslau, or the college-age students she had, later, at Speyer. One need only recall how calmly she could accept chocolate pudding as the main course for a meal at a girls' picnic which she chaperoned to know she would not be disturbed by any signs of youthful exuberance likely to surface in the novitiate.

The older nuns in the community remember that during her

time in the novitiate, Edith the postulant, and Sr. Benedicta, the novice, seemed to shed twenty years and to be a true contemporary of her youthful companions. When, with so much cause, she gradually became more and more serious in the later 1930s, her Sisters were consoled to think that for some years in Carmel, at least, she had tasted carefree joy and childlike light-heartedness, happy to be part of the warmth and love of a family of sisters.

There is a very natural interest about the demands "being in formation" put on Edith Stein, especially since she had been a professional for many years, and conventional methods of training in religious life had been structured for much younger persons with little experience of interrelationships outside their families. These conventional methods meant reading, daily lectures on the religious life, especially on the vows of poverty, chastity, and obedience. It meant living in a rather closed group with others in a formation "class", and learning to accept both directions and corrections with equanimity.

In most communities the method has been modified since Vatican Council II. Greater care has been given to suit the formation to individual situations, so that there is an adaptation according to a postulant's life experience, and there are few "general" practices such as were often hinted at, darkly, by those who had little personal experience either with the daily life of religious, or with formation programs. An accurate record needs to be kept of Edith's "time and circumstances."

The history of religious orders and congregations shows that zeal at times replaced discretion when the virtues were put into "practice" according to some of the old training manuals whether for men or women. One was supposed to learn humility by being humbled, patience by being assigned tedious or impractical chores and so on. Then, just as now, persons in a group were of differing temperaments and had their individual psychological equipment whether this was beneficial or painful.

But, to label all the practices in formation as harmful or insensitive is to beg the question. To consider that every correction was deliberately intended to inflict humiliation and pain would be a great injustice to those who had positions of authority in religious orders.

In 1933, when Edith Stein entered Carmel, Mother Renata

Posselt had charge of the novices. She was a talented woman with a strong but pleasing personality, experienced with those "young" in community, and she appreciated Edith's personal worth and her desire for Carmel. Mother Renata did not unduly set out to "test" the novices, for life in Carmel of itself provides sufficient material to keep one humble if one is honest. Since Sr. Benedicta had preserved every bit of the determination to seek truth which had characterized her youth, she frequently had an opportunity to experience her awkwardness in unfamiliar tasks, and this she did without evasion or self-consciousness. Once in a while, Mother Renata provided an extraordinary occasion for Sister Benedicta's practice of humility; she well knew that the senior novice would accept a correction in such a way that the younger ones never forgot it. These situations were neither belittling nor shaming. Of course, Sr. Benedicta *felt* a reproach as much as any of the others did; her respect for Mother Renata made some reflection from the superior even more distressing for this novice. And even in her teens, she said no one ever "corrected" her any longer.

Common knowledge in the Novitiate had it that Sr. Benedicta's needlework was good for little more than rudimentary repairs. One day, to everyone's dismayed surprise, the Mistress of Novices, upon examining one of Edith's efforts, mused as she handed it back: "Sister, I have heard tell how intelligent you were before you came here, but I do think you are now getting more and more ignorant."

Sister Benedicta was taken aback and rising color attested to her shamed feeling. As was the custom, though, she simply acknowledged the correction, took back the work she had presented to the Mistress, without bitterness or ill-feeling, and attempted to do it over in a more satisfactory fashion.

In Mother Renata's novitiate, the younger sisters were unhappy to hear Sr. Benedicta being corrected, but her acceptance and her unchanged attitude to her superior after the comment quickly restored their equanimity. Two of them, indeed, still remember how sincerely they wished they could be as calm when their failings were observed, and admitted trying to copy Edith's example for years.

18

Sister to Those You Gave Me

Often, during a study of Edith's spirituality, her own words on a spiritual evolution come to mind. She made the comment in a letter to Erna when the turmoil near the end of World War I seemed at its worst. She expressed her conviction that humanity was at a turning point in the "evolution in the life of the human spirit." She was certain enough to call it a "crisis" and declared her generation needed to be accepting of its position in history, contribute all it could possibly bring forth, and face the reality that the crisis might last longer than one was willing to accept.

When she expressed these reflections in July 1918, even Edith may have expected "humanity" to turn the corner before 1938. During those twenty years, three important turning points had been passed in her personal spiritual development. Her Baptism in 1922, entrance into Carmel in 1933, and her final religious profession in 1938 were as evolutionary as any progress made by humanity as a whole.

We have touched upon the effects and the significance of her entering the Church, and then of her acceptance in the Carmelite Order. When she made her perpetual profession of the vows as a member of the Cologne community on April 21, 1938, her own waiting in patience came to a completion. Every day in Carmel beginning with October 14, 1933, led up to this culmination, and every day, thereafter, including August 9, 1942, was a continuation of her commitment to the Lord, made on that day.

It must be noted, of course, that the "finality" of her profession in 1938 rested on canonical law. Her personal, internal, and psychological commitment to God, as a Discalced Carmelite took place on April 21, 1935, when she professed the vows of poverty, chastity and obedience at the conclusion of her year-plus-a-day of novitiate. On that occasion, her intention was to bind herself as a religious in Carmel for life. The Church, however, required that for three years, the vows be considered "temporary" as far as their binding force was concerned. The commitment of a woman or man, in the religious life, is so all-embracing that a three-year period is mandated to test the ability, will, and aptitude of the candidate, once the formative periods of postulancy and novitiate have been passed. The so-called "first" profession is made with the same disposition as the perpetual or final profession. The three-year duration is mentioned in the formula or contract, but at heart the gift to God is made "for life."

Once Edith, Sr. Benedicta, made her temporary profession on April 21, 1935, she entered another phase in her life in community. After their temporary profession, the Sisters are not yet admitted to full participation in community affairs, and they do not have a vote in elections. Since the renewal instituted by the Second Vatican Council, Carmelite nuns with temporary profession, and, indeed, novices and postulants, have a part in many decisions affecting community life. In Edith's time, these Sisters remained under the direction of the Mistress of Novices, but their status lay somewhere between that of the novices and of the chapter nuns. In the daily schedule of duties, however, there was little change to be noticed and life continued in common with the novices and postulants.

Principally, the new status showed up when the temporarily professed Sisters were called upon to assist newcomers and younger members in the community to learn the ropes, so to say. The better a nun with first vows had assimilated the responsibilities of a Carmelite in her own life and understanding, the more help she could give to the Mistress of Novices.

Because of her background, Sister Benedicta could be called upon for all kinds of assistance to her youthful companions in the novitiate. Her gift for languages, for one, was put at the service of the others.

Sister Maria Baptista related one incident to me in 1974, with detail and spirit which proved how lively the recollection remained in her memory. Nearly forty years had passed in the meantime; Sister Baptista had a new perspective on her own role in the story, and she told it with evident relish and amusement rather than chagrin.

Edith and this younger sister, who was still a novice, knelt one behind the other in the nuns' choir which had no pews. The Sisters knelt on the floor without support for hand or arms. The choir "stalls" were very plain, ranged along the wall, facing the opposite row for the choral recitation of the office. Edith, an excellent Latin scholar since her youth, had been reciting the Breviary for years and was very well acquainted with the psalms.

After they had been side by side for some weeks, Sr. Benedicta, senior in the novitiate because of her profession, approached the younger Sister and asked pleasantly, "May I make your charity aware of something?"

It was the custom before the renewal brought about by Vatican II to call one another "your charity" when speaking together. If one addressed the Mistress of Novices or the Prioress one said "your reverence." The purpose was, presumably, to guarantee that all were treated equally. Interesting, though, the experience of those who used this form of address. One was actually saying the same words when addressing different persons but one found they conveyed the various shades of friendship which existed. The human spirit has great resilience and finds ways to express itself. Sr. Baptista knew this was some "personal" remark being offered her. She said she looked at Edith a bit warily. It was unusual to have her come with such a question, and Baptista was certain it was with the permission of their directress.

With some hesitation, she nodded and awaited Edith's "remark."

"There is one word in Psalm 129 which you always mispronounce."

"You must be mistaken, Sister Benedicta, for I have my *vade mecum*, and I'm sure ... I can close my eyes and 'see' how it's shown there."

Sr. Baptista had made constant use of this small book which

was given to every sister at her reception into the novitiate. It instructed them in the pronunciation of Latin, a language totally foreign to most of them, although they heard it in church from childhood on. The small manual held something of a mystique for this particular young sister, she told me. From it she had gleaned what she was certain was a true proficiency at the Divine Office and she was proud of the achievement. Now, here was Sister Benedicta, not so far ahead of her in community, implying that something in the little book was incorrect. The idea amounted to near blasphemy in Sr. Baptista's estimation. Her defense of it, and roundabout, of her own pronunciation, of course, was anything but timid.

Even in 1974, one could tell from the expressive eyes what that interchange between the two Sisters must have been like. Edith, noticing the stalwart defense of the book, began to enjoy the discussion and assured her companion that book or no book, the word was pronounced differently, and repeated the correct version.

"I took my *vade mecum* out of my pocket at once, found the place, and showed her triumphantly that I had made no mistake."

Sr. Baptista recalled that by this time Edith's kindly amusement was plain to see, and the smile was in her voice as she explained there was a typographical error in the *vade mecum.*

The younger sister found it impossible to believe that her precious little book could contain an error and so she took the whole matter to the Mistress of Novices. Her chagrin at being told Sr. Benedicta was telling the truth was in no way lessened by the authority of the Mistress' corroboration. In her view, Edith had attacked the sacred little book.

With sad resignation, and some lingering doubt, Baptista made the correction as the Mistress suggested; her faith in the infallibility of the printed word began at least to waver!

After some years, of course, Sr. Baptista realized how amusing the whole incident had been, and she appreciated what the suppressed laughter meant for Edith who was so understanding of youth's idealism.

An incident like that, for a less sensitive person than Edith, might have become a story retold over the years with the naive Sr.Baptista as the target of the joke. That never happened, and had Sr. Baptista not told on herself, no one would have been aware of it except the Mistress of Novices. It was evident that Edith's respect for Baptista's feelings made a much stronger impression on the younger nun than the Latin lesson had occasioned. Whatever passed between Edith and any other, Baptista told me, whether it was a confidence entrusted to her or some sympathetic or helpful gesture on either part remained privileged, private information.

The kind actions were reciprocal, but it is significant that confidences were referred to only as being entrusted *to* Edith. She made confidential statements only to her superiors, and then, usually, they spoke about her deep concern for her ailing mother. To her Mistress of Novices, Mother Renata, who was elected Prioress eventually, Edith spoke freely of all her worries about her relatives, and about the possible repercussions Edith's presence in the community might have on the Carmel of Cologne.

In the summer of 1938, this question began to plague Sr. Benedicta more and more. It was increasingly evident to her from reports of her family in Breslau, and from newspaper stories, at Edmund Husserl's death for instance, that the Nazi government was serious in its program of elimination, although for a time the virulence of the disease rotting Hitler's party was festering under cover.

It is a frightful commentary that one can take consolation upon the death of someone as beloved as Frau Stein was for her youngest daughter. Yet, in the face of the Nazi terror and the experience of other elderly Jewish matriarchs of Edith's acquaintance, she found herself grateful that her mother's death on September 14, 1936, freed Frau Auguste from the enemy's harassment forever.

Perhaps the one reference Edith clearly makes to any inexplicable spiritual experience she had was about that September 14th. The day, each year, marks the commemoration by Catholics of the Exaltation of the Holy Cross. Allegedly, Helena, mother of the Emperor Constantine, discovered the supposed location of the Crucifixion on a hill outside of Jerusalem. According to the custom at such executions, the crosses upon which criminals had been raised were buried at the site. In any case, the discovery of the true Cross, and its being venerated because of its connection with Christ is memorialized on September 14th.

On that date, the Carmelite nuns began the "fast of the Order", a regimen limiting use of dairy products, though not as severely as during the "black fast of the Church" which was kept during Lent. The "black" denotes that the diet was free of all "whitemeats" a collective name for eggs, milk, cheese and other dairy products, all of which were avoided during Lent. This was the diet in Cologne which Edith followed in her five years there. Only during her postulancy was an exception made, when she was told to continue taking milk during Lent, although the black fast had begun.

By custom, bi-annually, on January 6 and on September 14, Carmelite nuns everywhere had a ceremonial, or ritual, Renewal of the Vows. This was in every sense a devotional practice, for the vows did not require "renewal", having been made to bind perpetually. The practice of repeating the formula, individually, in the presence of the Prioress and the whole community, was an opportunity to activate one's fervor. The determination one knew upon making the profession of vows the first time surfaced on such occasions.

Sr. Benedicta had experienced this ceremonial renovation of vows in September of 1935, again on January 6, 1936, the Feast of the Epiphany. On the morning of September 14, 1936, she went in her turn to kneel before the altar, to place her hand in those of her Prioress, and to pronounce the words:

> I, Sister Teresa Benedicta of the Cross, renew my profession, and I promise obedience, chastity, and poverty to God, to the Blessed Virgin Mary of Mount Carmel, and to you, reverend Mother Prioress and to your successors, according to the primitive Rule of the Order of Discalced Carmelites and our Constitutions.

When she spoke the words, Sister Benedicta had an unusual feeling that someone was beside her as she knelt before the Prioress. She had a very strong sense of her mother's presence at her side. For the moment, she put it out of her mind since at that very time, her mother was gravely ill in the large house on

Michaelisstrasse in Breslau. But the feeling was so extraordinary and so definite that Sr. Benedicta mentioned it to another nun when they had left the choir upon conclusion of the ceremony.

Later that same day, by telegraph, Edith was informed of her mother's death, and the time was precisely that at which Sr. Benedicta had renewed her vows and felt her mother's nearness.

In 1938, four days after her perpetual profession, Edmund Husserl died, and Sr. Benedicta was consoled that his death had somewhat of a link with her profession, just as her mother's had. She saw that as an answer from God to the many prayers commending her mother and her old-time "Master" very specially to his divine care.

When she wrote to a professor friend of hers who was acquainted with Husserl, Sr. Benedicta mentions a clipping from a Hamburg newspaper about the philosopher's death. He was Jewish by birth. Years before Edith met him, he had become a Protestant but that choice never obscured his ancestry. His great academic standing had not kept him from being hounded publicly by the SS, and it was clear from the newspaper notice which Edith labels "frighteningly cold" that he would not be spared under sufferance. Once more, she saw his release by death as a gift from the Lord. She need not worry about further suffering for him at the hands of the Nazis. The two persons whom she had held most dear were safely in the hands of God.

With perpetual profession, Sister Benedicta assumed all the obligations, privileges, and responsibilities of a chapter nun, a full member of the community. The symbol of her final commitment was the black veil of the professed, given her at a public ceremony on May 1, 1938 by Auxiliary Bishop Wilhelm Stockums of Cologne. Forty-nine years later, to the day, a huge photograph of Sister Benedicta wearing that black veil looked over the 70,000 or so persons gathered in the Müngersdorfer Stadium in Cologne for the ceremony in which Pope John Paul II, the Bishop of Rome, bestowed on Edith the title of "Blessed." For Catholics, this meant she could be honored in public, and her assistance could be requested in public prayer—she was assuming the obligations, privileges, and responsibilities of the men and women recognized by the Church as "blessed by the Lord."

In Carmel, in the years after leaving the Novitiate, Sr. Benedicta had filled several responsible positions in the community. But she is best known for completing in Cologne her important philosophical work on "Finite and Eternal Being." Five years earlier, her translation of St. Thomas Aquinas' *Quaestiones disputatae de veritate* had given her an insight into his doctrine. That translation also gives a student of Edith Stein a valuable insight in *her*.

In the 1920s, anyone in Germany who wished to study Thomas Aquinas' teachings had to know Latin. This was a handicap for many who would otherwise have taken the opportunity to learn from the Dominican's writings. Perhaps it is significant that a Jesuit, not a Dominican, induced Edith to undertake translation of Aquinas' "Disputed Questions." Edith had an excellent command of Latin; but as a neophyte, she felt she lacked the knowledge one ought to have if one sets out to translate one of the greatest teachers of Catholic doctrine. Father Erich Przywara, S.J., found that the pros outweighed the cons in Edith's case, and his persistence overcame her reluctance. The work appeared in two volumes in Breslau in 1931.

The translation caused Edith's name to spread in Catholic circles. A professor friend of her brother-in-law, Hans, told her she was being "talked about" in Rome because of the translation. Some German Dominicans expressed disapproval of the work, averring that it was not always an exact transmission of Aquinas' subtle distinctions. The reply Edith had for such comments is highly characteristic. She told them, frankly, she had expected to miss some of the great Doctor's nuances, but that having a faulty translation available in German seemed to her a greater good than waiting for one to be done perfectly. She also admitted to having had a suspicion that her work might spur some of the very learned German Dominicans to set about publishing translations of their own. This, too, had served her as an incentive; her expectation proved true. Dominican translations materialized in German.

The writer in Edith had many facets, and one which endeared her to her family, her friends, and very particularly to her sisters in Carmel was her gift of poetry. Again, we hardly find her achieving the stature of John of the Cross, or Teresa of Avila, in the quality of her poems. But she had her own greatness to give to the Order. A custom she began early in her religious life demonstrated her thoughtfulness. Few of the nuns in Cologne had a thorough knowledge of Latin. Praying the Psalms for many years had given them a vague awareness of the meaning of a few phrases. Vernacular translations of the Scriptures were still relatively rare in monasteries. Sermons were the usual source of information on the context in which the Psalms could be understood.

As each Sister's birthday came around after Edith's entry, she translated for her the Psalm bearing the number which corresponded with her age. There was enough disparity in ages for this custom to allow Edith a good number of Psalms to work with. When there were duplicate numbers of birthdays, she had other choices available. The numbers for years of profession were smaller than those representing age. The nuns treasured these translations and mourned losing them when an incendiary bomb set their monastery ablaze, destroying their books and personal belongings along with the building. It seemed a greater loss to them than their household goods— furnishings could be gotten, but unless they had learned their several psalms by heart, the translations were irreplaceable.

Light-hearted verses to celebrate feasts and anniversaries were also greatly appreciated. Unfortunately, here, too, little survived the fire of 1944. The wit and sometime sarcasm in this form of entertainment always had made Edith's contribution to family festivities the pièce de résistance at weddings and birthdays. For Erna's wedding in 1920, Edith conjured up an "interview" between the legendary Stork, manager of Babyland, you might say, and two prospective "babes", one of whom he was determined to reserve for Erna and Hans Biberstein. Gerhard, Paul Stein's son, kept his copy of the skit in which he portrayed the canny Stork. That copy enabled the Cologne nuns to preserve an example of Edith's flair for entertaining.

The dialogue between Stork and Babies is anything but predictable—it was 1920, after all. At the notion of being picked out without "representation" the two babies rebel. The young lady protests that she belongs to the Central Council for Babies' Rights, and cannot be coerced into going to parents she has been unable to appraise. The young man wants to be assured one gets fed to satiety. The Stork, unused to such back talk, blusters that he will simply deliver one or the other to these parents.

The sketch closes with an ending "fit for Edith" since Stork has won approval for the Bibersteins as prospective parents. However, the babies also win for, having heard the full argument, they *both* insist on going.

Edith had to repeat this story often at recreations in Carmel because the nuns enjoyed her gift of mimicry so much. Not only was this a perfect vehicle for her talent, it also seemed to show her prophetic skill, they teased. Every time there was news about the Bibersteins, there was reason to remember the skit since Edith had chosen a girl and a boy for Erna and Hans' family. She predicted correctly; Susanne and Ernst were as satisfied with their "choice" of parents as Stork had assured the tots in Babyland they would be.

These activities, the recreations and many other indications of a truly engaged life in community, show the external features of Edith's life from 1933 to 1938. A constant backdrop was her fidelity to prayer, and to prayer she took her increasing consciousness of the miasma of evil in the country.

Underlying daily life in Germany, coloring contacts from her former professional circles, there were strong, irrefutable intimations of a persecution of the Jews, of those who befriended or defended Jews, and of others who dared criticize or work against the N.S.D.A.P. (National Socialist German Workers' Party). Hitler had founded this party in Munich in 1925, and by 1938, the Nazis were powerful enough to wreak the inhuman depravity of Crystal Night, November 9 to 10. In Carmel of Cologne, the violence struck at the heart of Sister Benedicta who feared that her presence in the community would call down on the nuns the vengeance of the madmen.

Sister Benedicta, in the five years already spent in Carmel, had not changed her spiritual attitude. She was as ready as always to "receive everything from the hand of God."

It is absolutely necessary that we remember one thing she accepted from Him. Her intelligent, human, common sense which now told her she had to do everything possible to save herself and her community was a gift she recognized for all it meant. She had to take upon herself an active role in her destiny. It would not do to be passive, especially since some of her sisters were simply incapable of assessing the political situation and danger for what it was. It was unreasonable to expect that every last one of them would grasp all the ramifications of a world situation then, as it would be for us now to expect to know exactly what lies in store for us on the ecological or the political world scene in the next five years.

Edith, Sr. Benedicta, had long known how insidious the evil was. She had seen how blind some persons were, whether because of a cancerous national hubris, or a naive refusal to believe evil could be a national goal. The ability to blind oneself out of fear, or to refuse to admit responsibility for a situation we cannot face, was probably at the root of some of the ignorance claimed by those who should have been aware of what was happening in Germany.

The Nazi party had already interfered in education during Edith's last months of lecturing in Münster. Teachers, including Catholics, who expected to go on in their careers were required to declare themselves willing to comply with the regulation of *Gleichschaltung*. Simply put this meant they agreed to give up Catholic principles in their profession to take on those of the government.

Edith herself did not have to confront this question personally, since all opportunity of teaching had been taken from her. But her view on the morality of complying by Catholics was firm and unequivocal. It would be absolutely wrong. One young woman whom she had taught consulted Fräulein Stein and was told there could be no question of complicity with the government. The witness wrote: "When I said that a prominent cleric had said 'yes', Edith's reply was: 'This is not the first time that some of the clergy have to be "carried" by the laity.'"

Despite the immanence of trouble with the Nazis, Edith had prepared her class plan for the 1933 summer session, and her behavior was typical of one who was, in her secular circumstances, already conscious of her planned religious commitment. The spiritual aspect of teaching was so important to her that she planned a special course to give to the teachers at

Münster. In a "perspective sketch" she outlined the course for the next semester. She had, in past lectures, given them the "Structure of the (Human) Person" (*Aufbau der menschlichen Person*) and would now give them the whole thing again "but in the supernatural sense." Student-teacher Anna Hendker wrote of this preview: "Just hearing a short preview of the lectures overwhelmed me. I said to my neighbor in class: 'To think that there *are* such exalted and holy things! I've never even heard a priest *mention* them and here's a *woman* telling us about them.'

"I realized only later that she would have been giving us an insight into the mystical life. I was so taken by what she was saying, my heart and head were so much one in understanding what she told us that I stopped writing notes and just waited, like all the rest (of the student-teachers) with joy and impatience for the beginning of the semester. And it never came! She was never allowed to give another lecture."

As the risks she knew in Münster did not prevent her from planning lectures on spirituality which would defy the Nazis, so the increasing threat of their interfering with Carmel could not affect Sr. Benedicta's practice of prayer. Had the danger to the community not existed, she could well have elected to remain in Cologne. Her superior was in a very precarious situation also, principally because it was humanly impossible to estimate the safest procedure to follow.

19

Truth in Final Glory

"Where a soul listens in total surrender and uninhibited flexibility" to the Holy Spirit "and awaits His least wink," Edith wrote, "discretion will point out what needs to be done." As 1938 drew to a close, events affecting Sister Benedicta's life demanded immediate action. It is easy to believe that survival as much as discretion would have dictated urgency. Earlier, when the community had considered the advisability of her going to another community, Edith had expressed a preference for one of the Order's monasteries in Palestine. Several of the Chapter nuns found it impossible to believe that the risk for Edith, or for them, could ever become life-threatening. She, on the other hand, had a trustworthy sense of serious danger. But there was no chance of going to Bethlehem, a Carmel founded by French Carmelites in 1875, or to Nazareth, a more recent foundation, restored in 1919. The borders were closed by the British, just as those of other countries were shut to the increasing number of refugees as Nazi measures became irrefutably real to the most persistent of the hopeful.

It may be useful to remark once more that although so much of this account seems to be purely biographical, the real purpose behind recording it in this precise manner is to allow us today to realize what the spiritual atmosphere was like for Sr. Benedicta. We need to pay deliberate attention to the effect all these happenings had on her heart, mind, and spirit, and, once more, we need to depend on what we have learned about Edith Stein from her example, rather than on a record of her reflections. She left none.

About mid-year, 1938, the Stein family, at least Else's, Arno's and Erna's branches, began to move toward emigration. Arno's wife, Martha, and their children, Helmut and Lotte, were in the U.S. by July. Arno visited Edith on October 14 to say farewell on his way to join his family in America. Hans Biberstein was in New York, preparing as best he could to bring Erna and their two children to safety also.

Werner Gordon, Else's son, had been in Colombia, South America, for some time, and in December, 1938, his parents and one of his sisters were getting ready to join him. By this time, Edith knew her own destination. The nuns in Echt, Holland, were ready to receive her as soon as she could come. Rosa, Frieda, and Paul with Trude, his wife, were still in Breslau, where life became increasingly difficult for them.

Sr. Benedicta's departure from the Cologne community was difficult for her. She had come to regard these nuns as a second family, and she had a realistic intimation that her leave-taking was final; she would not return. There was no bright horizon for anyone to see; what mattered to her was that, once her leaving the monastery lessened the risk of retaliatory action from the Nazis, at least she could think of this family of hers as safe. That Cologne would be so badly bombed in the coming years was then far from anyone's mind in Carmel.

New Year's Day, 1939, was in every way a fresh beginning for Sr. Benedicta. It represented a break from the German nuns, but also from her relatives. While she was still in Cologne, she could have expected farewell visits from Erna and her children. Now, Holland made such calls impossible, for crossing the border created risks. Having waited so long for clearances, Erna prudently decided to forego a visit to Echt. At the time, none of them had reason to believe that the future would wipe out every possibility of seeing each other again.

Necessity had made her departure inevitable, but discretion decided the time, according to a letter from Edith during January, 1939. So far, no outside pressure had been put on the Cologne community, although official quarters were well aware of Edith's presence there. Many persons have conjectured that she should have been concealed and so kept safe from the Nazis. Had there been no proof of her departure for Holland, the community would have been under surveillance for concealing her. The requirement of all citizens to register arrival and departure from a locality with the police department was a custom of long standing in Germany.

Voting records were not the first indication the Nazis had of the presence of someone of Jewish origin in the Cologne Carmel. Dr. Edith Stein's reputation was such that her entry there had been widely publicized, and noted.

Far more decisive and important than the information the Nazis already had about her was Edith's own attitude toward concealment. She would have refused it in Cologne as strongly as she turned it down in Holland, when friends of the community there, especially the Jesuits of Valkenburg, urged her to go into hiding with their assistance. She took every measure that was legally available to emigrate, and she urged the nuns in Echt to the last moment of the last possible day, to seek permission for her to go to LePaquier, Switzerland, with Rosa. Indeed, a room in the Swiss monastery had already been made ready for Sr. Benedicta. But her principles, her standard for personal actions, ruled out every suggestion of her going underground.

Whether Rosa's situation might have influenced Sr. Benedicta's stance toward concealment cannot be proven. One can easily believe she might have accepted a plan of escape, other than emigration to Switzerland, had one been presented to provide safety for Rosa as much as for herself.

Her criteria for obedience, even to the occupation forces that had taken over Holland, are clear. She never hesitated to give witness to her faith and her pride in her Jewish heritage; she was not fearful of the Nazis, and refused to give the required salute to Hitler which, to her, was immoral. But when what she considered lawful restrictions put some transactions out of bounds, she was as firm in her determination to abide by the rules as she was in showing defiance when that was called for.

This singleminded pursuit of what was true for her caused her to make judgements about situations which, at times, understandably, differed from the view of the rest of the community in Echt. For some, it seemed to be a reflection on their own honesty; a narrow interpretation seems like criticism to those who favor a wide one, and the reverse is true, also.

Common sense provides us with insight about the positions in which both the nuns in Holland and Edith found themselves. As we saw when considering the criteria for acceptance of any Carmelite applicant, a great deal is ordinarily taken into consideration before a newcomer is judged compatible to a community.

In the case of Sr. Benedicta's transfer from Cologne to Echt, some factors must inevitably have created hardships on both sides, difficulties that are humanly speaking unavoidable, but which, from a supernatural viewpoint, were successfully met and overcome by all those involved, often at the cost of personal sacrifice. As one needs to repeat, frequently, admission to a religious group does not automatically change one's personal tastes and preferences. Nor can one always make the most perfect moves either in giving or receiving loving cooperation. Carmel is no more paradise regained than is any other human relationship. But those who were in Carmel, at Cologne and Echt, were, as Sr. Benedicta herself was, ready to follow the Spirit's "least wink." Again, because all were human, what was lacking was the ability in every single instance to *perceive*, to recognize, a wink from the Holy Spirit when it was given.

The unusual circumstance of accepting as a transfer someone whose very safety required her departure from Cologne added a dimension of urgency and nearly of inevitability to the positive decision of the Echt community. There must have been, just on statistical grounds, some nuns who had reservations about admitting a stranger from another country, even though she was of the same religious family. Sr. Benedicta, too, with her deep knowledge of human nature, must have realized that a transfer under the conditions in which hers was arranged meant that acceptance on both sides implied a willingness to put aside personal preferences.

Arrival in Holland meant studying another language, but Edith's giftedness made this a small hurdle. So proficient was she that before long she was able to take over the duties of the "turn-sister", an office she had held in Cologne. This responsibility kept her busy, for it meant that all contacts from within and outside the monastery were made through her, at the "turn", or at the enclosure door.

Eventually, Rosa Stein succeeded in reaching Echt. It was, however, only after a bitter experience which left her robbed of most of the personal items she had managed to get out of Germany through Belgium. A woman, in the guise of a sympathetic friend, offered all kinds of help to Rosa. As the result of the spontaneous trust Rosa reposed in this "warm-hearted Christian," who posed as a foundress of a new group of religious, Edith's sister came to feel lucky just to have gotten herself to Echt.

Rosa was made welcome at the Echt monastery where she lived and helped another laywoman in the extern quarters. Rosa would have wished, with all her heart, to wear the habit of an extern Sister, but the Superior thought it good to wait before taking such a decisive step. Just as in Edith's case, it seemed to the nuns that it was too soon after her Baptism for Rosa to join the Order.

There was no reason for her not to belong to the Tertiaries. Such membership could have been sufficient, had the Community been willing, for Rosa to wear a Carmelite habit, rather than secular clothing. Much to Rosa's disappointment, and to Sr. Benedicta's, also, the Prioress did not wish to have Rosa in the habit under the circumstances existing in Echt at the time. This decision had less to do with the fervent desire on the part of the Stein sisters than with the other laywoman who had served the Community for many years as an extern, without ever wishing to join the group or wear a habit. Were Rosa's wish to be granted, there would be a very noticeable difference between the two women who took care of all of Carmel's contacts with persons outside the cloister. This sensitivity to the older woman's feelings was reasonable, but one's sympathies are with Rosa who lost so much before she came to Echt, and for whom it would have been such a deep consolation to wear the same habit as her beloved youngest sister wore.

Edith's fidelity in prayer was noticed by the nuns. Not that this meant more than that her punctuality and absorbed attention were apparent to the rest, for there was little opportunity for longer hours than were scheduled when all the other nuns were at prayer, too. But the serious situation for all Jews gave added incentive and motivation to Sr. Benedicta's prayer.

The Nazi invasion of Holland was a calamity for all the Dutch, but doubly so for the Jews who had managed to find shelter there after leaving Germany. In many a case it was truly the fire which followed upon the frying pan. Regulations designed to harass those of Jewish birth were multiplied; and measures to humiliate and demoralize the Germans of Jewish background who had found refuge in the Netherlands were enforced to the embarrassemnt of the Dutch citizens who were unable to defend their guests against such hounding. Often, upon registering and receiving the "yellow star" which had to be worn, the victim was issued a letter listing dozens of towns and municipalities in the area which they were forbidden to enter even on a visit. Just to read one of these unbelievably inhumane documents has a humiliating effect on a person today; what must it have been like to know it was aimed "at you"!

In the Carmel of Echt, as in Cologne, the superiors recognized Sr. Benedicta's intellectual giftedness and set her tasks which, it was hoped, might distract her from the difficult situation for which there seemed no remedy. It must be said that Edith's writings in Echt are as careful, as intense, as scholarly as anything she wrote in Germany.

It was for the Feast of St. Joseph, March 19, 1939, that Edith composed a poem in which her understanding of the situation in Europe is clearly expressed. Taken from the Dutch memorial publication *Als een Brandende Toorts*, [Like a Burning Torch], the poem is both a prayer and a testimony of her faith.

SAINT JOSEPH, CARE!

Dark and heavy, the heavens loom o'er us.
Is night to be eternal, and light ne'er ours again?
Has our Father above turned 'way from us?
As by a nightmare's throttling,
　　our hearts are choked from need,
Is there no savior, near or far, who knows to help?
Behold, triumphantly, a beam bursts through the clouds.
With friendly gleam, a tiny star peers down,

Benevolent and mild like any father's eye.
And so I take all that affrights us;
Raise, and lay it into those steadfast hands.
              Receive it all—
              Saint Joseph, care!

Furious the storms which rage across the lands.
Oaks whose deep roots sank into earth's own heart,
Whose crowns soared proudly up to heav'n,
Lie now uprooted, rent asunder—
Horror, despoilment, round about.
Does not the storm shake faith's foundations?
And will her sacred pillars break?
Weak are our arms—who's to support them?
Pleading, we raise our hands to you:
You are, like Abraham, faith's own father,
Stalwart in child's simplicity,
   and capable of wonders,
In power of obedience, and of pure intent.
Protector of new Cov'nant's holy temple,
              Keep it safe—
              Saint Joseph, care!

When we must journey into foreign lands,
And, door to door, our shelter seek,
Walk then before us as our trusty guide.
You who companioned, once, the Virgin purest,
You, the Child-God's trustworthy, caring Father,
Bethl'em and Nazareth, Egypt, as well, shall be
A home for us, if you but tarry, too.
For where you are, there Heaven's blessing rests.
Childlike we pace our steps by yours,
Cling to your hands in perfect trust:
              Be you, yourself, our home:
              Saint Joseph, care!

20

Star and Cross in Eternal Light

In silence and hope some three years passed. Sr. Benedicta took part in the daily life in community as though all were normal. She saw Rosa in the speakroom regularly, usually on Sundays, and these visits were a source of strength and consolation to both. Persons not fully acquainted with the norms of enclosure which were observed in Carmel in Edith's time may be surprised that the Stein sisters, living in the same monastery, should be described as "visiting" with one another on Sundays.

Since she was not a member of the community, Rosa could not go in and out of the cloistered parts of the monastery unaccompanied. As extern help, she was permitted to work in the garden, but then she was admitted in the manner prescribed by the nuns' ceremonial. She came in to work, so conversation was limited to essentials. Although Sr. Benedicta, as "turn sister" was the one who opened the locked doors or gates through which Rosa entered the cloister, these occasions gave the sisters no opportunity to exchange any news or to inquire about personal matters. Ordinarily, family members visited the nuns only once a month, and for no more than one hour. The permission given to Sr. Benedicta to see Rosa in the speakroom every Sunday, then, has to be seen as an expression of the nuns' appreciation of Rosa's help, and as a means of giving both refugees some mutual consolation. In many ways, to have one's blood relative so near, and then, to observe the restrictions called for by the rule demanded a great deal from both parties. Such sacrifices, and the comfort which counterbalanced them, are an important commentary on these two Stein sisters.

That the country was also under occupation added to hardships for all the nuns. Rationing was stricter, if that were possible, than in Germany, and the nuns were fortunate if their vegetable garden furnished some supplementary items for their meager table. Naturally, in an occupied country, as much as possible was reserved for the military, or sent to Germany, and, as was the case almost worldwide, most staples became black market items. In this connection, an episode in Sr. Benedicta's life reveals her fidelity to truth in a very characteristic way during this trying time.

Little more than ten years had passed since Father Przywara had urged her to write down her memories of family life in Breslau. Edith began her journal, for that is what it amounts to, during the last weeks in her mother's house before she entered in Cologne. She brought the journal with her to Carmel and, during any free time in nearly five years, was able to continue writing the story of life in her family. She did not take the manuscript to Echt herself; the risk was too great. Her luggage would be searched for just such material at the border. Soon after her arrival in Holland, she realized she would have time and permission to continue this writing.

A plea went to Cologne, then. Was there some friend of the monastery who might be willing to bring the manuscript across the border? Someone not suspected of being even partly Jewish would surely run less risk of trouble. A young Marianhill missionary, Father Rhabanus, volunteered his help. He found his generosity put to a real test when the border police decided to search his automobile and one man picked up the bulky manuscript and flipped the pages. Luckily, he gave it no more than a perfunctory glance and dismissed it as "your doctoral thesis, evidently". The mysterious ways of providence!

Sr. Benedicta resumed writing the memoirs but had added very few pages by the time the Nazis invaded and took over Holland. Once more, she had to face the risk of endangering the nuns if a search of the monastery were organized and the manuscript discovered.

This was an important occasion in which Edith's spiritual attitude is manifested to us. The very circumstances under which the work had been started, its emotional investment for Sr. Benedicta, its ties to her beloved mother and the family now scattered all over the world, made the manuscript an embodiment of her deep attachment to her family. Its unique function of memorializing everyone's life during those years, now gone forever, gave it more meaning than it had ever possessed before. Now the question arose where to keep it so that it would not endanger the nuns were it to be discovered. Carmelite monasteries in Luxembourg and Germany had been commandeered; and the nuns had been compelled to leave with but a few hours of notice in most cases. Edith found herself with a problem she had never imagined would arise. After much thought, it seemed best to wrap up the manuscript as well as she could to preserve it from dampness and mold, place it in some type of container, and bury it on the monastery grounds. It would have become a very personal time capsule if it had been allowed to repose where Edith, with the help of Sister Pia, buried it in the vicinity of the nuns' private cemetery.

For some reason, Sr. Benedicta, according to the same Sister Pia, dug up the container some three months after hiding it. The cause for this change is not recorded anywhere, but, after years of acquaintance with Edith's story, and having observed her reactions in many instances, an explanation presents itself which is almost as dramatic as the hiding of the manuscript in the first place.

Like Carmelites the world over, the community in Echt used woolen material to make their habits, as this was required by their constitutions. And these constitutions carried no references dispensing from such regulations because of war. By 1940, woolen cloth seemed nonexistent. What there was, of wool or of any other material, was reserved primarily for military use. However, through channels known to friends of the community, a large bolt of material such as they had always used had been located and purchased at the black market price.

This was one occasion (others naturally existed but were of lesser importance) when Sr.Benedicta did not agree with the majority of the nuns who had anything to do with the purchase of the material. Her evaluation of their responsibilities was, as always, based on her perception of truth. Now, even though in her personal dealings with the Nazis she showed herself courageous and far from afraid, she never refused to comply with such regulations as were justified in her opinion. Whenever she had to report to the authorities, or if she had to submit applications, or rationing cards, she complied. When it came to giving the Nazi salute, even only in words, she refused; nor did she wear the star on her clothing until she was compelled to do so. These regulations were unjust; rationing, on the other hand, was a war-time expedient required in all warring countries, so that was an entirely different matter.

In the community discussions, it became clear that Sr. Benedicta did not approve of buying forbidden material on the black market. With the same reasoning as basis, she felt it was wrong to conceal the material in a hiding place which the other nuns considered an excellent choice. A large hollow tree on the nuns' property easily accommodated the bolt of material, and it was also readily accessible for the sister who had to make new habits for the nuns.

There was no possibility that Sr. Benedicta's view would be shared by enough nuns to make it an issue, but all of them were aware of her disapproval. What happened to the cloth, interestingly enough, remains a mystery, The nuns had to evacuate the monastery eventually and left behind almost all but the clothing they wore, However, recalling that Edith had buried her manuscript sometime prior to the purchase of the material, we now have a very probable clue to the cause of its being dug up.

When she realized that, clearly, according to her own lights, she considered concealing woolen material to be wrong, how could she any longer condone her own action of concealing a forbidden manuscript? This is an assumption, true, but how plausible! Sr. Pia, the only witness besides Sr. Benedicta, was not aware of Edith's motivation, in fact, she seemed to be puzzled about the manuscript's sudden "resurfacing". What Sr. Pia did record was Sr. Benedicta's quandary once she held her writings in hand again. "I cannot recall ever seeing Sr. Benedicta, or anyone else, appear so helpless! I went to her and told her to give me the manuscript for I knew a place where it would be safe."

Sr. Benedicta handed over the package without asking where it would be put, nor did she refer to it in the future. Since she had no opportunity ever to inquire about it, herself, it now seems a matter of providence that it was brought to Holland. Had it been left in Cologne indefinitely, the fire which destroyed the house would have consumed the manuscript. Its preservation for a time by methods which Edith reversed, once they appeared questionable according to her principles, shows us her human simplicity and her earnest attempt always to do her best.

Sr. Pia later said she found a hiding place for the manuscript somewhere in the house. When all the nuns were compelled to evacuate the building for their own safety, she left the manuscript in its repository, wherever that was, only to rescue it from danger of confiscation when the war was over, and the building was to serve temporarily to quarantine some two hundred workers repatriated from German labor camps. Sr. Pia came from a neighboring town where she was caring for one of the nuns who had been injured by a grenade, recovered the manuscript, and turned it over for safe-keeping to the provincial of the Discalced Carmelite Friars of Holland.

In the psalms we are reminded that "day unto day takes up the story" of our lives in God's hand. (Ps 19a:3) So, in Echt, in those final months and weeks of ever encroaching danger, there were the ordinary moments of daily living which passed as though all on the horizon was painted in the most promising colors. October 12, 1941, Sr. Benedicta's fiftieth birthday—the last she was able to observe with her Sisters—had been an occasion for particularly lively celebration. Little did the young religious know it was their final opportunity to regale their beloved Sr. Benedicta with "visitors from Old Testament times." That was, once more, a time for laughter till the tears came, for Edith wrote to a friend that the venerable "nose" of Moses was enough to put the entire community in awed admiration of his appearance.

Her work on the "Science of the Cross" must have been more difficult than any other assignment she had been given. After all, she was working on it at a time when sheer human frailty required extra stamina to ignore the constant uncertainty about her position and Rosa's. Once more, she feared that by harboring the Stein sisters, a community of women were being put in a dangerous position. Even the size of the building they were in proved to be a risk, for the occupation needed room for its oppressive forces.

All the nuns must have had a feeling of living in danger, and Sr. Benedicta, clear sighted far more than some of her sisters, must have known she could never finish the book on St. John. But her generosity is part of the greatness of her work. The manner of doing it, too, was typical.

She had translated St. Thomas, we recall, admitting her limitations but giving a scholar's reasoned opinion that it was better to provide others with a book that possibly was partially flawed than to deprive them of all source material whatever. Now, in Echt, she must have had a feeling of deja vu. Then, Father Przywara assured her she was capable of producing what he felt was essential. She obeyed him. Now, her prioress enjoined on her the writing of an essay comparable to those she had written so readily for "Master" Husserl's Yearbooks on Philosophy. She was to prepare a *Festschrift* on St. John of the Cross, to commemorate the Fourth Centenary of his birth in Spain, June 24, 1542. It need not be finished by the exact jubilee date.

The circumstances must have added up to frustration for Sr. Benedicta! Her assignment went side by side with continued troublesome demands from the occupation forces. On one hand she was asking other Carmelite Nuns in Holland to find her copies of the book on St. John by Father Bruno, the full 522-page volume, in French, published 1929, and one by Baruzi published in Paris, 1924. On the other, she and Rosa had to appear at the police commissioner's office in Maastricht because all "stateless" persons were to be deported by the end of the year. A person less disciplined would have told her superior to forget about a work she would surely never finish. But, again, to have some task actively absorb her attention was a distinct blessing.

She frankly admitted that Baruzi's book, with its lacunae, left her with more questions than information, and Fr. Bruno's book did not always provide answers that could be corroborated. It was a task from the Lord; that gave her all the assurance she required. She would do her best, and whatever the flawed outcome, He would, hopefully, make of it a tool for his creative hand in other lives.

That this is how she felt is deduced from her habitual attitude toward God. She did not need to put it into words, and we may safely say her confidence has been rewarded. The *Science of the Cross* deserves attention from the Order's experts on St. John of the Cross. Only they will know the great value of her independent lights on his doctrine. Wherever she was handicapped because of flawed or incomplete sources, they will be able to shore up her thought in a way which will present St. John from a viewpoint they themselves might never have conceived.

One learns the "science" of the Cross only when one has personal experience of "the Cross" through enduring the vicissitudes that come to everyone: this conviction of hers is as true as ever and applies as much today as in her time. The mysticism of Edith Stein will be understood by persons who practice it themselves. One who knows what it means to accept, and to accept once more, and never to stop accepting every successive moment of life, be it joyful or sorrowful, as something offered to us by a loving God, will know how to understand her life, and most particularly that final week of it which is shrouded in the greatest darkness and which, yet, illumines the lives of all who have heard about her since August, 1942.

Looking at the last months of Sr. Benedicta's life in the Carmel of Echt, one is reminded that one of the writers of Sacred Scripture likens God's intervention in our lives to the art of a weaver who severs the threads once the pattern has been completed. From her fiftieth birthday on, one might see in Edith's life a gathering together of the many threads as though to ensure there be no loose ends to spoil the masterpiece.

Faithful as always to her friends and family, Sister Benedicta, in 1942, time and again, received news which closed file after file in her memory's catalogue. Strict chronological order, once more, is dispensed with in order to see the final blending of colors and design come to completion. Since she wrote little to describe what we could call her personal spirituality, it is essential to observe the way she lived out these days for, with her honesty, her actions are a most reliable index of her attitude of soul. Yes, she was sad; indeed, she may have seemed less attentive to others, but she never stopped generously offering her assistance to any of the nuns, in whatever way it was possible.

A letter of Edith's from April, 1942, serves well as a frame in which these various strands may be examined and their worth evaluated. The letter is addressed to Fräulein Dr. Hilde Verene Borsinger in Bern, Switzerland. Sr. Benedicta was acquainted with Dr. Borsinger for many years; together they had tackled the problem of awakening women to their full responsibilities in society.

But this final letter had a different purpose. Dr. Borsinger was a jurist whose influence had opened Switzerland's doors to well-known Jewish refugees between 1939 and 1942. It was the eleventh hour for Edith, one arrived at through much pain and soul-searching.

Could she reconcile repeated efforts to gain permission to emigrate to Switzerland with her habit of allowing God to direct events in her life? Her prudence kept her from being mistaken in this situation. By giving her influential friends some years before their help would be needed in critical situations, God was as provident as if the solutions were all produced at the last moment. And it was not *his* will that the efforts should be nonproductive. God's will is often hidden from our human understanding even in the final resolution of a situation. When mankind has done its worst, God's omniscient providence still has ways of making the "best" of it for his loved ones. Only in eternity will we know how this was achieved.

Edith tells Dr. Borsinger that in the application for permission to leave Holland, submitted for herself and Rosa, the final destination was given as the U.S. This information was also sent on to her relatives "and to our provincial" in America.

That Provincial was Father Cornelius Leunissen, O.C.D., whose departure from Holland was precipitated by his appearance before the German police on behalf of the Stein sisters as far back as 1940. As an American citizen, Father Cornelius was himself harassed by the Germans. His decision to go to Maastricht, the regional headquarters for the Nazi occupation forces, was possibly foolhardy in the expectation that he would be permitted to intervene for Sister Benedicta because of her cloistered status.

Until that time, he had received more or less veiled threats of arrest as an enemy alien. When he appeared before the officer to report he was representing the Jewish-born nun who had been summoned from Echt, he learned how precarious his own situation had become. How dared a "Yankee" presume to plead the cause of a Jewess! He was ordered out of headquarters, and no sooner had he returned to the Carmelite Monastery of the Fathers than a loyal Dutch friend in the police department came to warn him that orders to arrest him in the early hours of the following day had been received.

Father Cornelius' friends prevailed on him to make his escape at once. Completely against his own wishes, he finally gave in to their urgings and made his way south through Europe to Spain from where he was successful in finding transportation to the United States. Sr. Benedicta hoped to let him know she had filed for permission to leave Holland for the U.S. via Switzerland, though she had little confidence in the success of her effort..

There is doubt that her letter ever reached the intermediary, Dr. Sieber, in Switzerland. He had been Hattie Conrad-Martius' family physician. These are the circumstances which since then have given cause for rumors that Edith sought an American Carmel for refuge.

In the letter to Fräulein Borsinger Edith mentioned that a Spanish Carmel had told her to come to them. (Inquiries have not yet disclosed which monastery was involved, nor how they came to know of her.) Travel was impossible, besides. All Germans of Jewish heritage living in Holland had been declared "stateless" and there was no chance of getting either a passport or a visa which would enable them to travel or to enter any third country. The Nazis were thorough in their hatred.

Now, the nuns of Spain were not the only Spanish Carmelites aware of Sr. Benedicta's plight. The Carmel of Echt was under the jurisdiction of the Order. The prioress was the superior in the monastery; the Provincial of the Fathers in Holland was next in rank, and all the provinces of the world were under the Father General whose headquarters were in

Rome. It was customary for the Superior General to visit the various provinces during his term of office.

With a war of the magnitude of the Second World War raging, to leave the Generalate in Rome to travel throughout northern Europe because of his personal concern for the friars and nuns reveals the calibre of Edith's highest superior, Father Peter Thomas (Sioli) of the Virgin of Carmel, O.C.D.

On July 26, 1942, the very Sunday on which the fateful pastoral letter of the Dutch hierarchy was read aloud in the parish churches of the Netherlands, he arrived at Echt. His coming brought the nuns comfort and new courage because it was such a tangible reminder that there are loyalties and commitments that go beyond war. A rare break in the everydayness of life was also welcome.

In the company of some of the Dutch Discalced Carmelite Friars, Father Peter Thomas spent some hours with the community. Already acquainted through correspondence with Edith Stein's story, he made it his concern at Echt to inquire of Sr. Benedicta whether the situation was under control. He specifically asked what her personal preferences were regarding a permanent transfer and what she would like to do. She told him she would like most of all to remain right where she was, in Echt. For one who, at that time, had friars and nuns under his jurisdiction in all of the warring countries, the predicament in which Sr. Benedicta found herself would have had particular urgency and he was determined to help her achieve her goal, once he learned her own wishes.

Had Edith wished at all costs to get to Switzerland, she could now have made this known to Father General in person. In some ways this direct contact could have greatly facilitated the process of transfer. Not only was permission required from the secular authorities; as a strictly cloistered nun, Edith needed acknowledgment of her situation from her Order, as well. The Rule contains the wise caution: "Necessity has no law." Technically speaking, then, as there was so much danger, formal permission could have been dispensed with through the General's directives on the spot.

Because so many records were destroyed by fire and bombs, it has not been established whether, regarding a further move on Sr. Benedicta's part, the Dutch superior, knowing of the imminent visit of the General, had saved the entire bureaucratic problem for Father Peter Thomas to solve. With so serious a matter to settle, the General would have made certain that Echt was included in his tour of visitations just then.

The danger from the Nazis in Holland was so real that the juridical steps which had to be requested from Rome for a permanent transfer from Cologne to Echt had not been forwarded although the requisite positive vote from both Chapters had been given. The delay would have been for Sr. Benedicta's benefit. If permission from the country of Switzerland arrived, she could be transferred at once (on official records) from Cologne to LePaquier.

In bureaucratic terms that would have meant saving months of delay, and days of paper work. As a Carmelite Nun with perpetual vows, the "stability", or state of belonging to one monastery rather than to another, did not deprive Sr. Benedicta of any of the rights belonging to a permanent member of the Order. It was a matter of deciding which Monastery granted her these full rights at a given time. She was never "abandoned" by her Order, and some of the rumors about "betrayal", or "abandonment", must be due to misunderstanding the procedure followed when such transfers occur.

One would have to search the general archive of the Order to get an idea whether Father Peter Thomas was still in Holland the following Sunday when the SS took revenge on all the nuns and priests of Holland who were Jewish by birth. His years as superior general were saturated with anxiety. Humanly speaking, it is tragic to realize that just as the burden had lightened a little, Father Peter Thomas, during a pastoral visitation to the Friars in the southwestern province of the U.S., was fatally injured in a terrible automobile accident near Santa Fe, New Mexico, only four years after meeting Edith. The foreign necrology records the fact in remarkable fashion: "he died August 28, 1946, in Shamrock, U.S.A.".

So much for human intervention for Sr. Benedicta and Rosa. Even with so many persons involved, there was no success.

In all the multiplicity of her duties at this time, she was struggling with a single, enormous task: how to balance what *she* had to do, either as a religious, or as an alien being harassed by inimical officialdom, with her practice of accepting everything from the hand of God. Passive activity, or active passivity; playing with words defies the reality of the situation. We see her, day after day, taking up her self-appointed task, picking up what she had laid down at the throne of God the night before, and carrying the burden, actively, for the space of one more day, making whatever spontaneous sacrifices this entailed, and enjoying any of her Divine Master's gifts which He might hand her along with her work.

Having put all things in order, each in its sphere and time, we come to the final scenes in Edith's, Sr. Benedicta's, days. The support that came to her from following the regular daily schedule must not be overlooked. There were extraordinary events within that final month at Echt which caused her great pain. Word was received on July 28 that her brother, Paul, his wife Trude, and their sister, Frieda had all been arrested and sent to Theresienstadt. There, they too died as victims of the Nazis within a year of Edith's and Rosa's death.

The final week of July, 1942, brought the whole question of finding refuge in Switzerland to the fore again. A letter from Mother Marie Agnes, O.C.D., from Le Paquier contained the long awaited affirmation that Rosa, too, would find shelter with the Third Order Carmelites whose convent was an hour's drive from the Swiss monastery. Sr. Benedicta's response to Mother Marie Agnes, in French, was dated July 24.

The coincidence of time between LePaquier's assurance of a welcome awaiting them, Father General's visit two days later, and Sr. Benedicta's and Rosa's arrest on August 2, explains the flurry of efforts on the part of the nuns at Echt, a Red Cross nurse from Amsterdam, and Edith, herself, who wrote a telegram from the camp urging the prioress to make one more attempt. It was far from a matter of having waited until now to make any serious efforts. The favorable reply from Le-Paquier was a renewed incentive for one final many-pronged stab for freedom. If God saw it for best, one of these would take hold and secure a lifeline.

These synchronous events on several levels at this time dispel any suspicion that among those at Camp Westerbork, the Steins were expecting special consideration from the Red Cross or the Swiss Consul. It was clearly the sensible, responsible action of anyone to whom a hand is extended; making every effort to grasp it still does not mean one has succumbed to fear. Had Sr. Benedicta been terrified, she would hardly have been able to write as calmly as she did, requesting action as soon as possible on their permits to leave the Netherlands. This opportunity for a final attempt was also accepted from God.

The perversity and evil will of men determined to deny the human rights of others whom they considered expendable did *not* come to Edith from God. It is a mystery, but still a certainty, that evil has no root in and no causality from God. But neither has it power to thwart his goodness and his care of his own. Only a Divine Being has the capability to convert chaos, caused by the corruption of deliberately evil, human will, into a new scenario, infused with a manifestation of his infinite love so that it results finally in a masterpiece of beauty and happiness for the victim of injustice.

The eyewitness accounts of Sister Benedicta's actions in the camps, of her quiet, patient acceptance of the humiliations which the captors were already inflicting on their prisoners at this time, are no surprise. What may be unexpected are her references to being "wholly at peace, and cheerful." One is reminded of Dr. Edith Stein, eminent lecturer and writer, at the time she became a postulant in Carmel. She could lay aside all her professional sophistication and become a "child in her father's house".

At Westerbork, she had an analogous experience. Suddenly she was freed once more from planning her own moves. She could revert to her favorite stance before God, accepting without trying to foresee what the next moment might bring. By concentrating on a last landslide of appeals, she had satisfied whatever obligation remained to get herself out of the situation. Now, she could pick up her essential work which not even arrest by Nazis, or detention, transport and harassment, might affect. She could give herself to the prayer of readiness, of acceptance, of a *fiat* to all that was still unknown.

This release from the need to direct her future enabled her to devote herself to the children at the camp who were being neglected and left to their own frightened devices. Parents and

adults were crushed by the painfulness of the past, the uncertainty of the present, and the impossibility of conceiving the
future. Sr. Benedicta's past and future were all part of God's
present which He now shared with her, as she preferred, one
moment at a time. What was her prayer during these days?

Since her reticence to speak of the most intimate of her
feelings had always kept her silent, her prayer has been examined through cautious observance, always conscious of
having to make assumptions based on externals. We look for
the same kind of evidence about her prayer in her final week
of life.

From her note to the nuns we have some information in her
own words: naturally, they have had to do without Mass or
Communion, but that provided them with a small experience
of what is means to live entirely out of the center of one's
being.

The support and source of substance for her personal prayer
life had always been the liturgical prayer of the Church. When
she and Rosa were arrested, her breviary was among the few
articles she managed to take with her. On the other hand,
clearly she had not thought of taking along her food rationing
card. She mentions living on the charity of others until hers
could be forwarded, so, evidently, the prisoners had to surrender rationing cards even in Westerbork.

At the direction of the camp authorities she asked for
blankets and clothes, which were then confiscated when they
arrived. She added her own request: that the next volume of
her set of Breviaries (needed by the end of August) be delivered
to Westerbork. She seemed to expect to be sent either to
Silesia, or Czechoslovakia, and it would be better to have
someone bring the third volume to her at the camp than to
risk not having it when it was going to be needed.

On August 6, in her final letter from Barrack 36 to Mother
Ambrosia at Echt, Sr. Benedicta tells her prioress, in paren-
theses, a thought she just *had* to share with her superior
because she herself was so filled with it: "so far, I have been
able to pray, gloriously."

What did this mean? Certainly her prayer was not an endless
pleading for deliverance for that would hardly have qualified
for the term "glorious." Perhaps, from the Breviary for that

week, we may get a glimpse of the arms which sustained her prayer, as the arms of Moses had been supported in the most crucial battle of his life.

The first six days of August marked the celebration of some feasts especially dear to her heart. How deeply she had pondered the story of "Peter in Chains" when the angel of the Lord liberated Peter by severing the chains that fastened him to sleeping guardsmen! One of her letters calls attention to this episode, making her feelings on it clear.

The intervention of angels in the history of humanity was something in which Edith Stein believed strongly, probably even before her Baptism. The Breviary lessons and the prayers in the Missal for August 1st would have formed a basis for meditation on her own need for the company and assistance of God's angels. Because of her Jewish heritage, she would also have been aware that on the same day, the seven, courageous, Maccabean brothers were commemorated in the Catholic Church for their fidelity to their faith in the one, true God.

August 5 and 6, Our Lady of the Snows, and the Transfiguration, were also feasts which provided a wealth of deep consolation and strength as she prayed the Office during her detention in Westerbork.

In some sense, these are assumptions about the nature and content of her prayer. However, the Sr. Benedicta described by visitors to Amersfoort and Westerbork is so much the familiar, strong, and pleasant nun we know that the question arises: from where did her strength and cheerfulness come?

Such an intelligent woman, informed by the manifold experiences of her fifty years of life, had at least to think the end of that life might be near. The rumors heard in Münster nine years earlier had not been forgotten. During the years in Echt, in following the yearly liturgical cycle attentively, she had many an occasion to advert to the meaning of life and of death, and to consider how, during the one, she would prepare for the other. In her last will and testament, we find the formula familiar in the history of Christian spirituality: I accept now the manner and moment of my death. This is a positive attitude toward life. Though she might be robbed of that life, she could not be deprived of her dignity even in the face of degrading measures inflicted by her captors. Surely, during this final week, the many ways her life in Carmel had prepared her for a total act of returning all to God came to her mind, like methods learned in survival training.

This was a battle she had prepared to wage, even though she had not known, and was still not totally certain, where and against whom it would be fought. Had she contracted tuberculosis, like Thérèse of Lisieux, her "plan" would have been the same: to accept all from God.

Adrienne von Speyr pointed out that Edith's was, at the end, a triumphant prayer, the grateful cry of one whose faith in God's Truth has been rewarded and who has been liberated beyond the reach of all her enemies. Whatever they may do to her, she will be taken safely into the Kingdom of her Spouse, and there she will be forever his.

The final paragraph of Adrienne's description of Edith's prayer must be recalled because of its great relevance. When Dr. Edith Stein entered the Carmel of Cologne, she laid aside her secular renown and became, in a sense, anonymous by choice. At Auschwitz, where she was made one of the faceless millions, she was seemingly deprived of the last vestige of human dignity: her personal identity. Adrienne points out that, although "entering into an even greater anonymity crowns her mission as she bears the presence of Christ to the extreme place of suffering, the principal accent of her mission (still) rests on her vocation as a Carmelite, even more than on her martyrdom."

Witness to this is offered as a final *plaidoyer* for Edith's "only message". When one is able, with the total sincerity and fidelity which she reached, to live *at the hand of God*, then even in the forecourt of death, one can live as Adrienne saw Edith living "in triumphant certainty that everything is perfectly simple and unequivocal. She will pursue the path God is showing her: she belongs to Him; through love, through faith, she has found again her childlike happiness which has now been augmented and become self-evident" in peace and trust in God.

If we have recognized ourselves in any lines of this portrait, then blessed shall we be, and grateful to one whose example can be followed in every walk of life: From God, to God, all in His Hand!

On Bibliography and Sources for this Study

This work has benefitted from the research required for the translation of Edith Stein's unfinished autobiographical account *Life in a Jewish Family*. The archives of the Carmelite Monasteries of Cologne and Tübingen, Germany, as well as of Echt (in 1975) and Beek, Holland, were opened to me. Correspondence and conversations with family members gave many insights into the situations Edith described, and research into letters from her former friends and students rounded out the picture. It must be stated that there are still other avenues to pursue in the study of Edith Stein's life and times, and much needs to be translated and published before one can "know" Blessed Edith, the woman and the Carmelite, with an approximation to the knowledge the Order has of Teresa of Jesus, or Thérèse of Lisieux, for instance. There are several choices for preparing a bibliography. The one finally decided upon is a list of her own writings, in German, which are the basis of this work, in varying degrees. Always, by preference, the German version was used; when possible, as for the "Mystery of Christmas" and other direct quotes, the archival material preserved in the Cologne monastery was used. Since the study was intended to introduce readers to the person and personality of Edith Stein, the emphasis has been on her character rather than on her writings. Popular biographies of her are available; these and books of devotion are not listed in this bibliography because their number will increase and vary. The works by Edith herself, now available in German, need to be listed so that scholars and students of spirituality will know what can be expected, and by contacting the sources listed, it will be possible to learn when new editions in English become available.

The works are listed by their German titles with an English equivalent appended. When the works eventually come out in English, the publisher may have a varied title, but it will be possible to note which work has been translated.

Titles marked by an asterisk are known to be in process of translation, or may appear soon as publications of the Discalced Carmelite Fathers of the Washington (D.C.) Province through their Institute of Carmelite Studies. Minor works in English, generally devotional, appear from time to time, as publications by American or British Carmelite Nuns, or as translations of German books or articles by the nuns of the Cologne and Tübingen Carmels. Information, and usually, copies, of all of these materials are available through the Edith Stein Guild in New York, NY.

Edith Stein's Writings

Ten volumes published as *Edith Steins Werke* are:

1. *Kreuzeswissenschaft* (The Science of the Cross)

> This volume appeared in a translation by Hilda Graef in 1960. For the time being, it is out of print.*

2. *Endliches und Ewiges Sein* (*Finite and Eternal Being)

> Edith subtitled the work "an attempt at an ascent to the meaning of being" and she says it is addressed "from a learner to co-learners". The book was completed during her years in the Cologne Carmel, and was in galley proofs at the time when publication of any book by a Jew was proscribed. The German edition finally appeared in 1950; a second was published in 1962; a third, by Herder, in 1986, in time for Edith's beatification the following year.

> Again, Edith herself describes it as a study of the relationship between Thomas Aquinas' teaching and Edmund Husserl's phenomenology. She was encouraged to tackle this subject by the Jesuit, Erich

Przywara, who had been instrumental, earlier, in her translating Cardinal Newman's Diaries from English into German, and Thomas Aquinas' *Quaestiones Disputatae* from Latin into German.

This major work will be welcomed by all students of Edith Stein when ICS offers it in English translation.

3 and 4. *Des hl. Thomas von Aquino Untersuchungen ueber die Wahrheit* (St. Thomas Aquinas' Inquiries on Truth)

These two volumes present Edith's translation of *Disputed Questions* by Thomas Aquinas. Although these "Questions" seem not to be available in English, it is unlikely that Edith's work will be translated in entirety, as it would mean presenting Aquinas's work after a double redaction into a language he did not use. However, it would be rewarding, when the other original works have all appeared in English, to have Edith's clearly marked digressions, or glosses, in these two volumes, also made available to her English-reading public.

5. *Die Frau: Ihre Aufgabe Nach Natur und Gnade* (Women: Her Task according to Nature and Grace).

This volume, translated by Freda Mary Oben, Ph.D., was published by ICS Publications (Institute of Carmelite Studies, 2131 Lincoln Road, NE, Washington, D.C. 20002) in 1987 as *Essays on Woman.*

The lectures presented in this volume were given to Catholic women in Germany, Switzerland and Austria. Written half a century ago, they contain ideas timely to our present day situation, and those in need of adaptation can easily be updated. The motivation and spirituality underlying the topics presented are as valid today even when implementing Edith's suggestions calls for evaluation in our post-Vatican II era.

Critical Documentation
On Page XXXVII of the fifth volume of Die Frau in German, the lecture given in eighth place on "The Tasks of the Swiss Catholic Academic Women" is described by the editors as consisting of nine single sheets, a carbon copy of a typed, undated, unsigned work. The editors designate it as "in all probability, the draft of her [Edith's] lecture in Zurich."

Immediately following on Pages XXXVIII and XXXIX, is found the text of six pages of an undated manuscript, signed by Dr. Edith Stein (Münster i.W.), in her own handwriting, entitled by her: "Mission of the Catholic Academic Woman." The editors state that from signature, paper and handwriting they conclude this short piece has a connection with the address given on pages 219-226, inclusive, in the book.

Investigation postdating publication of the German edition by 28 years, and of the English translation by several months has established the proper identity of the authors of the two manuscripts as follows.

a) The shorter piece on pages XXXVIII and XXXIX was written by Edith as reflections on a manuscript she received from Dr. Hilde Verena Borsinger of Luzerne, Switzerland.

b) Dr. H.V. Borsinger is the author of the lecture found as Chapter 8 of the English translation published in 1987 i.e., the second volume of the Collected Works of Edith Stein by ICS of Washington, D.C. A letter from Dr. Borsinger to that effect, also stating that Edith Stein, herself, never spoke on this topic in Switzerland was personally verified in detail by the executrix of Dr. Borsinger's estate from documents in her possession.

It is expected that future editions of Edith's writings on Woman, whether in German or English, will carry an appropriate reference to this inadvertent credit of authorship.

6. *Welt und Person: Beitrag zum Christlichen Wahrheitsstreben* (World and Person: A Contribution toward a Christian Striving for Truth).

This collection of six of Edith's minor works contain her essays on: the worldview of phenomenology; a study of nature and super-nature in Goethe's "Faust";

Edmund "Interior Castle"; Martin Heidegger's existential philosophy; and her own study of the ontic structure of the person. Two of these, on Teresa and Heidegger, were appendices to "Finite and Eternal Being", originally. Perhaps they should become available in their original positions; but as part of the collected writings their contribution will be valued in either volume.

7. *Aus dem Leben einer Jüdischen Familie* (Life in a Jewish Family)

Released in 1986 by ICS Publications (Washington, D.C.) as the first volume in the English language "Collected Works of Edith Stein", translated by Josephine Koeppel, OCD.

For many reasons, particularly the need to keep the present work on Edith Stein's *Way* as a mystic appropriately short, no mention has been made in this smaller work of events and persons whose importance in Edith Stein's life must not be overlooked. Her own words, in both *Life in a Jewish Family* and *Woman* are essential for understanding her contribution to the world and to the Church in her own time, and, especially, in ours.

8 and 9. *Selbstbildnis in Briefen* (*Self-Portrait in Letters)

These two volumes in German contain 349 letters written between 1916 and 1942. A third volume of letters to appear in German is in preparation and it is hoped that all the letters can appear in chronological order in a translation remotely in preparation at this time.

11. *Verborgenes Leben* (*Hidden Life)

This volume appeared in German in 1987. It is a collection of minor writings treating of the Carmelite Order; pray in the Church; hagiographical writings written by Edith at the request of her superiors; meditations on the Cross; and reflections on the vocation of a Carmelite.

These works vary in interest as well as in importance. It must be pointed out that the hagiographical works, especially the one on a French Carmelite, Sr. Marie-Aimée, are written in a style which is no longer in use for biographies of persons venerated for their spirituality. To have written an assignment in another style than the one Edith used, would have been as little understood in her time as the style found here is appreciated in our day. If one reads beyond the expressions, one finds worthwhile material for an appreciation of a generous and spiritual person who was loved and admired by her sisters in Carmel.

There are several minor works in the Edith Stein Archive in Brussels which have not yet appeared even in German. Since the beatification in May 1987, a concerted effort is being made to get these works into print. It will be noted that Vol. 10 of the German Collected Works is not listed here. It was written by Fr. Romaeus Leuven, OCD and tells the rest of Edith's story, beginning where Volume 7 ended. It is not described here because this bibliography is restricted to the writings of Edith Stein, personally.

If Volume 12 of the German collection is to present the balance of letters which have been collected since Volume 9 appeared, it is hoped that subsequent volumes will make available Edith's writings on: an introduction to philosophy; the constitution of the human person; on anthropological theology (or theological anthropology); her essay on act and potency; on a maternal art of education; also a number of shorter inspirational writings on vocation and spirituality. These last unpublished writings are listed in the report released by the official theological censor of the Congregation for the Cause of the Saints.

Other Published Works of Edith Stein:

a) Zum Problem der Einfühlung (*On the Problem of Empathy)—Parts II and IV of Edith Stein's doctoral dissertation.

An English translation by Waltraut Stein, daughter

of Edith's nephew, Gerhard, was published by Martinus Nijhoff, The Hague, in 1963; a second edition appeared in 1970. Through ICS, the work is once more available in a revised paperback edition.

Surprisingly, some students need to be reminded to read this dissertation as the work of the graduate student, Edith Stein, not of the Carmelite. It will have interest for psychologists as well as philosophers, even for those who simply want to observe Edith Stein's thought process. Like her other works, it proves how thoroughly she considered her topics, bringing to bear every possible consideration.

The Niemeyer Publications

In a letter written in August, 1919, Edith Stein speaks highly of the publishing firm of Max Niemeyer—"the ideal publisher, really, and they belong right in the family of the phenomenologists." When a *Festschrift* was planned, to celebrate Husserl's 60th and 70th Birthdays, for instance, it would be Niemeyer in all probability who would publish it. They now have three of Edith's minor works. essays for these commemorative volumes, available in German re-editions.

1. *Beiträge zur philosophischen Begründung der Psychologie und der Geisteswissenschaften:*—(*Contributions on the Philosophical Foundation of Psychology and the Arts*)—*reprinted from the Yearbook, Volume 5, 1922.*

2. *Eine Untersuchung über den Staat* (Inquiry into the State)-from the 1925 Yearbook for Philosophy and Phenomenological Research, edited by Husserl.

3. *Husserl's Phänomenologie und die Philosophie des hl, Thomas von Aquino. Versuch einer Gegenüberstellung* (*Husserl's Phenomenology and the Philosophy of St. Thomas Aquinas. An Attempt to Compare Them.) Printed in the 1929 *Festschrift* honoring Husserl's 70th birthday.
These essays again demonstrate the careful thought of

Edith Stein and the breadth of her knowledge. Making them all available to English readers should be given a high priority.

An American Contribution:

Ways to Know God—written specifically to be translated for the American counterpart of the Husserl Yearbook, in 1941, after Husserl's death. The German title was *Wege der Gotteserkenntnis* and Edith sent it to her friend, Fritz Kaufmann at the University of Buffalo. It was translated into English by Dr. Rudolf Allers, a personal friend of Edith's, and the article was published in the *Thomist,* Vol IX, No. 3, July 1946.

The article was reprinted and is available in booklet form from the Edith Stein Guild, Inc. (60 William St., New York, NY 10005.)

This essay presents Edith's reflections on the teaching of Dionysius, the (Pseudo)-Areopagite, his "Symbolic Theology." It is a cherished legacy for American readers since it was written particularly for them.

Subject Index

abandoned by God, 21

Abraham, 28

academic: union, 89; women, 51; world, 129

acceptance, 19; active - of all from God, 24, 27, 74, 90, 100, 107, 124, 139, 152, 153, 168, 169, 173, 174, 177; grateful, 67; - refused in Carmel, 94

actions confirm attitude, 37. *See also* consistent.

active ministry, 74

Adenauer, Konrad, mayor of Cologne, 102

adolescence, 25; pre-, 26

adult, education should prepare, 41

Africa, 55

Allers, Dr. Rudolf, 185

Alsace-Lorraine, 60

Als Een Brandende Toorts [Like a Burning Torch], 160

America(n): citizen, 169; emigration to -, 151, 156; newspapers, 90, 155. *See also* Carmel.

Amsterdam, Holland, 173

angel(s), 16, 176; arch-, 98

Antwerp, Belgium, 9

Aquinas, Thomas *See* SAINTS

Arch: abbey, 75, 130, 132, 135; abbot *see* Religious: Walzer; -bishop of Cologne, 102

aristocracy in Carmel, 131; in Spain, 133

articulate soul, burden of, 34

assimilation ass Carmelite, 93

atheist, self-styled, 26, 55, 78

attitudes, confirmed by action, 37; - of others, 68

Aus dem Leben einer Jüdischen Familie See Literature

Auschwitz, 91, 177

Austria(n), 42, 51, 59, 85, 86

authenticity, 65; - of call, 74

Avila, Teresa of *See* SAINTS

Bach Festival, 44

bafflement, 109

Barrack, 36, 175

Baruzi, (Jean), 167

Basle, Switzerland, 79

Batzdorff *see* Biberstein

beatification, 14, 66, 129, 149

Becker (Minister for Science), 62

Belgium, 9, 159

belie (f,-ver), identified, 67, 82. *See also* faith.

Benedictines *See* RELIGIOUS

Bergzabern, 70-72

Berlin, Germany, 62

Bern, Switzerland, 169

Bernanos, (Georges), 78

Bethlehem, 15, 22, 161

Beuron, Germany, 75, 122, 130, 132, 134, 135

BIBERSTEIN: family, 152, 156;
- Erna, 30-3, 35-7, 49-41, 52-3, 66-9, 76, 151
- Hans, 52-3, 69, 150-51
- Ernst Ludwig, 76, 77
- Susanne (m. Batzdorff, Alfred), 76, 77, 82

Bibliography, 178-185

Bismark (Otto von), 102

black market, 163, 164

Blessed *see* beatification, Edith Stein, Saints.

emigration, 157
energy, physical and psychic, 112
enclosure, 93, 103-05, 134; - regulations, 107
Endliches und Ewiges Sein see Literature
endurable: to ourselves, 23; making oneself - to God, 81
enemy alien, 170
enjoyment, 33, 146. *See also* joy
entrance ceremony, 104
environment, 42
Episcopate (R.C.) of Holland protests, 171
eremitic life, 120
escape, Carmel is not an, 94
estrangement from God, 21
Eucharist. *See* Sacraments
Europe, 9, 97, 113, 123, 135, 160, 170
Evangelical (Lutheran) Church, 55, 69
evil, 16, 17, 174
evolution of the human spirit, 68, 143
exile, religious in, 102
experience(s), 33, 35, 36, 41, 42, 46, 68, 72, 93, 112, 123, 125, 134, 141, 175, 176; near-religious, 44; spiritual, 147
exterior life, 22
extern: quarters in Carmel, 93; Sisters, 159

faith: change of attitude to -, 50; - conviction, 94; father of -, 28; in action, 26, 66, 68; in God, 38, 59, 78, 84, 176; life correspond to -, 76, 80, 85; lost 25, 26; "of her fathers," 25; role of -, 26; - shared, 66; shield of -, 96; - tested, 65, 93; witness to -, 123. *See also* GOD
family: fidelity to her, 77, 168; interrelations in -, 25, 40, 50, 54, 66, 69, 77, 87, 96, 104, 128, 132, 163; love of -, 45, 164
fast: and abstinence, 138; black -, 148
Father's house, in her, 74
fear, 36; - blinds, 153; grave -, 94
FEASTS:
- of Booths, 97; Circumcision of Our Lord, 26, 74; Corpus Christi, 83; Day of Atonement, 30; Exaltation of the Cross, 147, 148; Good

Shepherd Sunday, 129; Our Lady of the Snows, 176; Peter in Chains, 176; Presentation of the Lord, 26; Saint Joseph, 160; Saint Teresa, 74, 104; Transfiguration of Our Lord, 176
fidelity: to faith, 176; to truth, 37, 50, 65
Finite and Eternal Being see Literature
flexibility to the Spirit, 155
formation in Carmel, 119ff
France, 85
Frankfurt-am-Main, 57
fraternities: drinking in, 43
fraud, an impediment, 94
Frauenwaldau, 31
freedom, 19: of choice, 94; of will, 68
Freiburg-im-Breisgau, 51, 54, 60, 61, 66, 67, 69, 70, 84, 86, 92, 130
friendship(s), 54, 57, 58, 66, 68, 69, 93, 99, 109, 129, 130, 131, 133, 168; misunderstood by, 25
Frings, (Joseph) Cardinal, 102
futility of voting, 89
future, worry about, 19

Germany, 10, 12, 28, 30, 42, 49, 59, 62, 69, 84, 86, 101, 102, 114, 120, 123, 131, 135, 137, 150, 159, 160, 163, 169, 170, 174, 176, 177
Gleichschaltung, 153
GOD (includes references to CHRIST and the SPIRIT): 10, 11, 18, 19, 21, 48-50, 59, 69, 70, 72, 89, 92, 97-99, 105, 119, 123, 128, 148, 155, 176; did not exist for Edith, 78; the Divine Master, 73, 92; kept treasure for her, 75; mercy of, 131; relates to Edith, 25-27, 29, 30, 34, 58, 71-4, 79-81, 106, 122, 124; love exclusively, 106; -' secret, 20, 28, 73; truth found in, 25, 34, 65. *See also* JESUS; living at God's hand
Goethe, 42
golgotha, 17
GORDON, ELSE, 32, 36, 38-40, 53, 98, 156; Max, Dr., 39, 40; Werner, 156
Göttingen, 45, 48-52, 55, 59-62, 64, 66, 68-70, 83, 84, 92, 110, 130, 138
government regulations, 62, 101
Graef, Hilda, 179